"An unexpected combination of bibli⟨...⟩
What Cannot Be Lost exposes the raw⟨...⟩ ⟨...⟩ ⟨...⟩
the same time, applying the only effective salve. Simply put, it's one of
the most honest books on grief I've ever read."
Amanda Bible Williams, Co-founder, She Reads Truth; General
Editor, She Reads Truth Bible

"The things that happen to us in life—whether things of gain or loss—
become meaningful through the stories we tell about those things. The
story Melissa Zaldivar tells in these pages finds meaning through the
frame of the beautiful stories she has immersed herself in: the stories of
Louisa May Alcott, the stories of people she knows and loves, and the
truest and best stories of all—those of the Bible. *What Cannot Be Lost* is
a beautiful testimony to the power good stories have to make our lives
better, even (or especially) when we face great loss."
Karen Swallow Prior, Author, *On Reading Well: Finding the Good
Life through Great Books*

"Good writing is observation, and Melissa Zaldivar does it best. She's
careful with these tender stories of loss and wise in showing how they
weave together. *What Cannot Be Lost* is a stunning book for every heart
that aches to make sense of grief and longs to believe in a beautiful
future."
Lisa Whittle, Author, *The Hard Good*; Bible Teacher; Podcast Host

"As a man who's had his world fall apart in a single day, I can attest to
the all-sufficient God, who heals and refills a broken heart and provides
his all-sufficient love in the most creative of ways. God was certainly
creative in how he brought Melissa Zaldivar into my life. In my darkest
season, she helped me see God's all-sufficient love and helped me look
for God in the midst of my mess. Allow her to do the same for you."
Jonathan Pitts, Author; Speaker; Widower

"*What Cannot Be Lost* is a masterpiece of tears, belief, and the boring grit of the daily. Zaldivar's writing, somehow both panoramic and immediately accessible, is the best kind of weird and the most captivating sort of ordinary. Here, the plain truth is a comfort. Here, grief coexists with delight. Here, Jesus and Taylor Swift whisper from the same page, and we find ourselves more human and closer to God. You will love this book."

Shannan Martin, Author, *The Ministry of Ordinary Places* and *Falling Free*

"*What Cannot Be Lost* was a labor of love for Melissa, putting words to grief. It is a kind and gentle companion, full of the type of empathy that can only rise up out of walking through deep loss and being comforted by the Man of Sorrows himself. With honesty, Melissa kindly nudges those walking through grief to collapse into the strong arms of Jesus and find belonging and comfort, even in the pit."

Ellie Holcomb, Singer; Songwriter; Author, *Fighting Words*

"Just as Melissa guides tourists through Louisa May Alcott's historic home in Massachusetts, she gently leads us through the shadowy corners of our own grief, ever reminding us that we are never alone. There is a tremendous depth of comfort in Melissa's words that can only come from a soul who has experienced profound loss; each chapter is a quilt to wrap around a weary heart. *What Cannot Be Lost* is a profound gift for any soul feeling the terrible sting of grief."

JJ Heller, Singer/Songwriter

"When grief wraps itself around the goodness in our life, we often feel suffocated by senselessness. Melissa Zaldivar has an uncommon way of giving words to the unspeakable parts of our lives, and by doing so, she frees us to breathe again. This is a book we need."

K.J. Ramsey, Licensed Professional Counselor; Author, *This Too Shall Last* and *The Lord is My Courage*

"It is a beautiful thing to form a friendship with an author from another time and find comfort in their story. Hand in hand with the century-distant Louisa May Alcott, Melissa Zaldivar walks through rooms of grief and promise to find what cannot be lost in the sad days and strange nights of grief. Beautifully told and heartfelt, this book bears witness to a friendship and what it means to give voice to our grief."

Sara Groves, Singer/Songwriter

"I read *What Cannot Be Lost* with tears running down my cheeks. It helped me release the stored-up grief in my soul as I found comfort and a companion in Melissa's honest reflections on loss. When sorrows threaten to overwhelm us, when death of any kind casts a shadow on our lives, *What Cannot Be Lost* is the reminder we all need to know that we have a God who stays with us in our weeping and who loves us to—and even beyond—the end."

Grace P. Cho, Writer; Speaker; Poet

"Divisive times call for decisive messages, and I believe Melissa has such a message within her. If there's something we can all agree on in this post-pandemic period, it's that our lives have been annotated by grief during this time. In every margin, we read the story of hopes dashed, dreams deferred, and loves lost. In these times, we turn to the things that comfort us the most, and for millions of people, the work of Louisa May Alcott tucks us into our beds and nurses us back to health. What better guide could we have than Melissa? A bridge between our sisters in Orchard House and modern grief, she is the perfect person, with her own insights on grief and grace, to thread the needle that begins the painstaking work of mending our hearts. These stories are timeless for a reason, and she knows them intimately. *What Cannot Be Lost* is so, so, so deeply needed after this past year."

Erin Moon, Podcast Host; Writer

"From the creaky floorboards of Louisa May Alcott's Orchard House, Melissa Zaldivar coaxes forth a story both tender and true. The very best of tour guides, Melissa infuses history with contemporary relevance and leaves us feeling as though we've come to know Louisa's heart like a friend's. *What Cannot Be Lost* reminds us that loss will touch us all; but in the midst of sorrow, divine Love endures with a beauty that death and grief cannot destroy."

Clarissa Moll, Author, *Beyond the Darkness: A Gentle Guide for Living with Grief and Thriving after Loss*

MELISSA
ZALDIVAR

WHAT CANNOT BE LOST

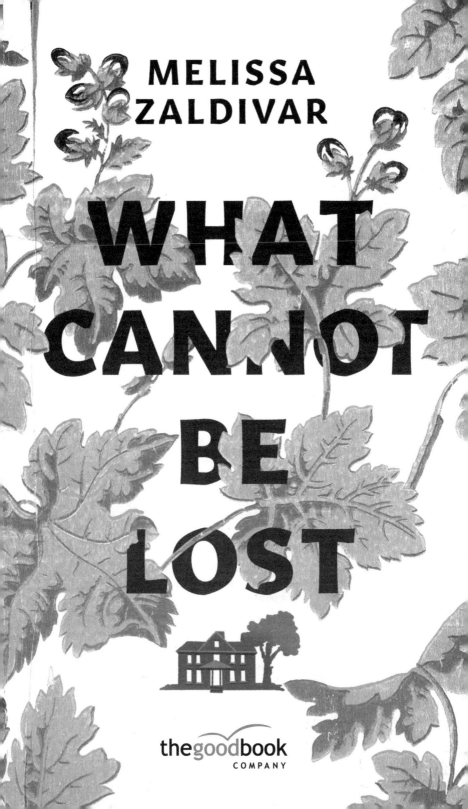

thegoodbook
COMPANY

What Cannot Be Lost
© Melissa Zaldivar, 2022.

Published by The Good Book Company

Published in association with the literary agency of Wolgemuth & Associates

thegoodbook.com | thegoodbook.co.uk
thegoodbook.com.au | thegoodbook.co.nz | thegoodbook.co.in

Cover design by Jennifer Phelps | Design and Art Direction by André Parker

ISBN: 9781784987640 | Printed in India

To Jillian Christina Joy Gudim:
I stood with you on your wedding day, and I can't wait to see
you again at the Wedding on the other side

"We might die, but we don't die forever."—Jennie Allen

"Therefore we do not lose heart. Though outwardly we are wasting away, yet inwardly we are being renewed day by day. For our light and momentary troubles are achieving for us an eternal glory that far outweighs them all. So we fix our eyes not on what is seen, but on what is unseen, since what is seen is temporary, but what is unseen is eternal."
—2 Corinthians 4:16-18

Contents

FOREWORD

By Bethany Barnard

I remember when the hospice nurse first showed up at my parents' house. The garage suddenly wasn't just for the lawnmower and Dad's handyman supplies, but a hospital bed, a lift, and an oxygen tank. We'd had a month to prepare; it was right before Easter, at the beginning of the pandemic, when the doctors said they had reached the end of the road of treatment. Dad had been fighting stage four cancer for the second time in a decade. The first time, he miraculously went into remission. But, as options started dwindling and his cancer spread, the hope of a happy ending slowly faded to silence.

The nurse left a pamphlet on the kitchen counter titled, "When the End Is Near," which gave a rundown of what happens to the body—signs to look for—as someone slowly slips away. I leafed through this tangible proof that it was the end, feeling more in denial than I ever had, and I wondered why I had no idea about any of this stuff.

I'd probably heard about it, but it wasn't the same as living through it.

Witnessing it.

Powerless to slow down or speed up or alleviate any part of it.

Powerless to protect myself or anyone else from the pain.

Words like hospice or cancer or chemo aren't one-dimensional to me anymore. They are triggers: vacuums that pull me back into those moments that are simultaneously a blur and never-ending. I have an involuntary, visceral reaction when I hear them. I am transported back to those days in 2020 before and after my dad died.

It's like moving out on your own for the first time, or the stage of life right before marriage or becoming a parent. You have a lot of information, advice from others, stories—you feel adequately prepared. And then... you're figuring out how to get your water turned on or how much appliance repairs cost, or realizing that no one else is going to make appointments for you or get your phone bill paid on time. Or you're married, and suddenly it makes sense why your vows say, "... in sickness and health, for richer or poorer; as long as we both shall live," because the actual living out of those promises is no cake walk. Or you're a parent, and a full night's rest is a cruel joke. You're up at midnight, and 3:00, and 4:00, and 6:00, just trying to keep this fragile person alive and not lose your sanity in the process.

After my dad's death, I was angry and broken and empty. The constant fuel of adrenaline and updates was gone, and I was not ok. It was hard to pray. Hard to listen to worship music. Hard to be in groups of people who were talking and laughing and going on with their lives. In my grief, I began looking for lament in the Bible, in songs, and in books. I longed for companionship, camaraderie, and being known in the place I was in. I still do. Maybe you do, too—and maybe you have found, like me, that those places of refuge are rare.

I read *What Cannot Be Lost* and felt the comfort of someone who knows. I was invited into Melissa's and Louisa's stories and was given an opportunity to examine my own. Reading this book is finding the gift of being understood. I felt as though I was having a conversation, not reading a page. It is a sacred thing to be invited into someone's loss. It's a kind of hospitality when they open the door and let you into the lowest moments, searing pain, and resounding trauma. Here, Melissa goes first; and it creates space for you and me to be a questioning, grieving, hoping mess, too.

I so appreciate that Melissa does not attempt to tie a pretty bow on it. I bet you're tired of Christians doing that, too. I'm grateful that she bears witness to the one who cannot be lost—and won't let go—when the dark times come. He's there. We're not looking for some harrowing story of heroic faith but one about how Jesus stays when we are falling apart.

Maybe you've been looking for something like this. I was. This book, these pages, this conversation is a safe place for you to not be ok. The shadow won't last forever, and you aren't alone.

Bethany Barnard

A Note to Readers

The world of literature overlapped with reality in the case of Louisa May Alcott, one of America's most influential authors. She famously wrote about what she saw in her real life, in the mid to late 1800s, inviting others to find common ground in shared experiences. Because there can be, at times, a blur between literary characters and the very real Alcott family, we offer you this helpful guide:

Abigail May Alcott: Also called **Marmee**, Abigail was the matriarch of the Alcott family, the kind and hard-working mother of her four daughters. Her maiden name, May, was the inspiration for the fictional March family, as March is also a month that begins with the letter M.

Bronson Alcott: Bronson was the father, portrayed in *Little Women* simply as Father or Mr. March.

Anna Alcott Pratt: The eldest of the Alcott daughters, Anna was represented in *Little Women* as **Meg**. She married John Pratt and had two sons: Freddy and Johnny Pratt.

Louisa May Alcott: Louisa was the second born and writer of the family, author of *Little Women* (among many other books), and wrote herself into the story as **Jo**.

Elizabeth Sewall Alcott: Elizabeth had the most nicknames in her family. She went by **Lizzie, Betty,** and, most famously, **Beth**. She was the inspiration for the third sister of the family, Beth, whose death has influenced readers for generations.

Abigail May Alcott Nieriker: Named for her mother, May Alcott was the youngest daughter and a well-known and celebrated artist. If you rearrange the letters in her name, you get the name of her character in *Little Women*: **Amy**. She married Ernest Nieriker and had one daughter, aptly named Louisa May.

CHAPTER 1

The Process of Losing

"Every memory is biased," she said with kind eyes. I was sitting in a counseling session, trying to figure out which of my feelings were "legitimate." So much had happened over the last year and a half, but as I emerged from it, I found myself critical of my own experience, wondering if I was even allowed to be that upset. Was it really as hard as I remember? Did I see things accurately, or was I somehow blinded by my own imagination? "There's no such thing as a totally perfect memory because you only see it from your perspective," my counselor said with a reassuring nod, "But the feelings are real."

When you've walked through the kind of story I'm about to tell you, it can feel a bit maddening, and you have to be compassionate with yourself. Someone always has it better; someone always has it worse. I don't know what weight you're carrying into these pages—what experience or heartache or hard conversation is taking up so much room in your heart. But when we try to make our stories of grief and pain and loss make logical sense, we can often rob ourselves by making comparisons and talking ourselves out of the reality of what went down. We cheapen our grief when we try to rationalize it away.

Much of life is paddling in and out of memories. It's making our way out on the water in calm conditions or stormy weather, but always coming back to the same harbor and anchoring ourselves in Truth. Sometimes it's a song or a word of encouragement that pulls us back. Making rhythms that move us in toward Christ has a way of slowing us down when our minds start racing. God's word and the narrative in it isn't just a tale we're told and cannot relate to. It's the compass that guides us and reminds us to keep moving along—despite doubts, imperfect memories, and darkness—toward light. And things had been very dark.

So I'll start with the start.

"In the beginning, God created the heavens and the earth."
(Genesis 1:1)

I know. This is really the beginning. But it's important because when I become the most untethered, this is what I go back to. It's like hitting the reset button in my heart. I take a moment to look in the mirror and say, "Let's go back to when creation was new and things were right and retrace our steps."

In the book of Genesis—which literally means "beginnings"—God creates everything. Every star and critter and plant and mountain and hillside and river. Everything seen and unseen. And then, once the earth is filled, he makes humans in his own image. They have perfect communion with him, but all of that changes.

The first man and first woman sin, tearing apart the perfection surrounding them, and the literal Eden they are living in is ruined.

They are crushed, but God does not abandon them. No, he promises in Genesis 3:15 that even though it might seem that all of the light has gone, he will send a Savior who will defeat the dark because he will be the Light of the world (John 8:12).

This is the hope that we cling to, and we're not the first, last, or only ones to do so. The Bible is full of people who found themselves in darkness, but kept coming back to that promised hope. In fact, thousands of years after creation, a shepherd who became king of Israel, named David, wrote what would become one of the most well-known passages of poetry in history. This is what he said in Psalm 23:

> *"The LORD is my shepherd; I shall not want.*
> *He makes me lie down in green pastures.*
> *He leads me beside still waters.*
> *He restores my soul.*
> *He leads me in paths of righteousness*
> *for his name's sake.*
>
> *Even though I walk through the valley of the shadow*
> *of death,*
> *I will fear no evil,*
> *for you are with me;*
> *your rod and your staff,*
> *they comfort me.*
>
> *You prepare a table before me*
> *in the presence of my enemies;*
> *you anoint my head with oil;*
> *my cup overflows.*
> *Surely goodness and mercy shall follow me*
> *all the days of my life,*
> *and I shall dwell in the house of the LORD*
> *forever."*

These verses have been heard—and memorized—by countless people. They paint a beautiful picture of peace and still waters and pastoral scenes, but then the attention of the psalmist gets a little more somber as he writes about "the valley of the shadow of death."

In the original Hebrew, this can also be translated as a "valley of darkness and shadow of death and dying." So, it's a real upper. I heard that verse as a child, and I remember not liking that part because it felt far away and overly dramatic. Of course, at that point, my primary distress was that I had washed a Giga Pet in my jeans pocket, which, of course, rendered it useless.

But as time went on and life got more complicated and things got truly dimmer, those verses started to hit different. An all-encompassing shadow known as grief had crept in and was covering every corner of my world. We've all had moments where we just can't catch a break, but this was a series of losses that threatened to end life as I knew it and offered no comfort of getting any better. Just when I began recovering, something else showed up like an unwelcome guest at my door.

It started when a friend died on my birthday that summer.

I turned 30 and I got the call hours before I was going to sit down to dinner and blackberry cobbler with friends. I told them all to come anyway because I didn't want to be alone, and they were gracious when I cried through the evening surrounded by charcuterie and their kindness.

The following month I lost my job due to budget cuts. As a single woman trying to pay off student loans, make rent, and stay afloat financially, this was a worst-case scenario in my mind.

A few weeks after that, I got a text from Jill, a beloved friend from college.

I don't know if u are awake or not, but I need some serious prayer for my health tonight.

I sat up and read it again.

I could hear the desperation in her voice as I read the request on my screen. I felt angry that I'd gone to bed early

WHAT CANNOT BE LOST

and couldn't respond right when she sent it. That morning, we started walking an 86-day journey from guessing to knowing the outcome of her sickness. From uncertainty to the understanding that she was going to die.

Just a few months prior, I'd driven a U-Haul across the country to Massachusetts, where I was still settling in near the Atlantic coastline. It was a long-awaited move to a place where I could stay after years of moving around the country, but the thrill of a hopeful future was cut short when things started to fall apart. The shock of so many losses that summer left me in a daze. It felt like everywhere I went, I bumped into grief. My own, my community's. It was like being perpetually sunburned—tender on every surface.

Maybe you've felt that sore, fragile sort of way. Words are spoken or a diagnosis is given and suddenly the colors turn and the tone changes, leaving you lost and wanting to lie very still, avoiding anymore contact with the world around you.

As the losses stacked up, I got used to the ache of never feeling totally at peace. I made a habit of waking up and tell myself things like, "The first few hours of the day don't count" because I was so often overcome with fear or anger or uncertainty that made me want to give in and crawl back into bed.

But it was summertime. Everything was bright and warm and flourishing, except for me. I didn't feel like the birds that sang or the fireworks that lit up the sky or the joyful picnics after a day at the lake. I felt myself disconnecting from the world around me because my own pain wasn't reflected on any surfaces I could see.

Sometimes it's easier to get quiet and distant until something else brings you back to earth. For me, it was the day I stepped into the dining room of Orchard House. It wasn't my first time visiting the place where *Little Women* was written—I had passed through before, the way that tourists do. I'd seen the 1995 movie and grew up with the nostalgia of that film, but this trip was different. I was seeing it through new eyes. Sitting quietly in Concord, Massachusetts, this brown house has become an icon to those needing to be reminded that our stories matter. Its halls are soaked in the story of four sisters who all grew up within its walls—sisters that live on through the timeless tale of Meg, Jo, Beth, and Amy March. Standing there that afternoon in early autumn, the space felt different. No longer seeing it as a random historic site, I found that it suddenly felt intensely personal. I looked around at the Alcott family's paintings on the walls and their china in the cabinet. And it was as if I was beholding it for the first time, weary and war-torn, waiting to hear what was to come for Jill.

There are very few places where I have physically stood that bore witness to specific moments in history that hit right at the core of my personal life. One was the Mount of Beatitudes in Israel where Jesus said, "Blessed are those who mourn" (Matthew 5:4). Another was a hillside, near where I live, which was one of the sites where the Great Awakening was preached. And now, lingering in the dining room of Orchard House, surrounded by the belongings of the Alcott family, I could almost see Louisa pacing around, trying to find the right combination of words for the chapter she was working on and the emotions she was working through.

I imagined her grabbing a snack in the kitchen because she was putting off the inevitable task of putting pen to paper. She was intensely disciplined but also hit ruts and got stuck in the swamps of writer's block. This ground is familiar territory for many of us writers or creatives, and we know the terrain well. But she was on a whole other level of commitment. For example, Louisa taught herself to write with her left and right hands so that she could go on for up to 14 hours when inspiration struck: a "vortex," as she called it.

She was unusual, and so was the house.

The Alcotts were far from wealthy, and this house was a last-ditch attempt at stability. Orchard House was the 29th house they'd lived in, and Louisa wrote as a way to make money and help keep the family in one place. She swore in her journal that she would see to it that the family stayed put for 20 years. So she took up residence at the desk that sits between the two front windows of her bedroom and scribbled out everything she could imagine. It worked. They stayed in Orchard House. But her greatest story was still unwritten.

Back then, they didn't have storylines like *This Is Us* or *Parenthood*. Storytelling was almost entirely fiction or fantasy. In fact, lay theologian G.K. Chesterton once commented that Louisa was a pioneer of realism (that is, writing books about real life) decades before it rose to fame. She was ahead of her time but even so, she was certain that a story about her sisters wouldn't sell. Nevertheless, she sat down at her desk and told us about how four girls grew up. About how one got married and how one traveled the world and how one published a book and how one died too young.

Ten years passed between when her second youngest sister Elizabeth (Lizzie) died and when *Little Women* was written. Orchard House was where Louisa sat for a decade as her grief steeped into something she could swallow.

I wonder if she, too, sat with her feelings and tried to figure out how legitimate her pain was. I wonder if, after seeing the horrors of the Civil War, she said to herself, "My memory may have deceived me and I guess my losses weren't so bad." Just like me sitting with my counselor, Louisa often undercut her own struggle and lost compassion for her own story in the face of uncertainty.

And maybe that's why I felt the most at home there. Orchard House moves at the speed of not knowing. It honors the past while being unsure of the future. And if there was one thing I was feeling, it was unsure of the future. Aching for some normality in my job search, I took a part-time position giving tours of Orchard House as I did the full-time work of coping with loss.

There are a thousand different ways that people experience the sensation of losing. It can be absolutely devastating and throw us off balance, but it can also be like a low hum in the background that you start to get used to over time.

Sometimes grief is simple and short. Like a dinner party getting canceled or a date being postponed. Not the best, not the worst. We'll make it.

Other times it's like a slow-rolling summer storm: dark and sticky. The kind of thing you call the dog inside for. But unlike a storm, we very rarely spot grief on the horizon with enough time to take cover. People can tell you that they see it coming, but they are usually making that up to help themselves feel better. We occasionally spot a moment of sadness in the distance, sure. But we are never actually prepared for how it knocks the wind out of our lungs. For the way it lingers. For the stiffness in our muscles afterward, or the way it comes back when you are least expecting it.

This is not a book about how to avoid or expedite your grief. There are not seven simple steps to finding immediate victory. There are not three easy ways to be #griefproof. In fact, when we look to Scripture for examples of grieving people, they abound. Barren widows and prodigal sons and abused servants all find their way to God, and it's hardly ever clean-cut.

Mary Magdalene followed Jesus closely and saw with her own eyes his miracles and believed fully that he was her hope. And then, on a dark Friday, she stood there in absolute shock as he hung on the cross, with heaving chest and outstretched arms. She witnessed him suffocating to death, and when his body was removed from where it had been hanging, she felt his dead weight pulling her down. In the following hours, in silence, she paced back and forth, face wet with tears as time dragged on. Appetite lost, she thought about the way he had been able to feed thousands. Breathing shallowly, she thought about how his nearness had allowed her to fully exhale.

On Sunday morning, she found her way to the garden tomb where he had been buried. It was the only thing she could think to do. She just wanted to be near him, even if he wasn't alive. Like wearing the sweater of a loved one or holding on to a necklace that they once wore, she wasn't ready to admit that Jesus was gone.

Imagine her shock and horror when she discovered the stone that covered the tomb was rolled away and all that she found was some linen—and no body.

Head spinning, she turns and starts sprinting, tripping over herself. Her eyes go blurry as she fights back tears of fresh lament, and she comes to the house where Simon Peter and John are, and she barely gets out the words, "They have taken the Lord out of the tomb, and we do not know where they have laid him" (John 20:2).

They push past her and start sprinting to the garden together, overcome by the idea that someone has had the audacity to steal the body of the friend they've just buried. Everyone is sweaty and scared and confused.

As the shock wears off, they go back to their homes, defeated. But Mary stays, weeping. Puffy-faced and snotty and out of peace, she just stands there, her breath a visible vapor that lingers in the morning cold. She is alone.

Until she's not. A voice asks her why she's crying and she starts telling the story that she's been reliving in her head for the past three days. About how she came to the tomb and he wasn't there anymore.

He wasn't there anymore.

He wasn't there anymore.

Her head hangs low in despair when, suddenly, he speaks her name, and she looks up.

She's so certain that her eyes are deceiving her; she can't even fathom it could be him. She doesn't remember the feeling of hope. And that's her state until he finally makes it clear that he is alive again. Not a big sunrise moment of shouting and light and victory. He is found in the early morning humidity, standing beside a traumatized woman who can't pull herself together.

Grief is in part what makes us human. It exposes to us what's already there. It wounds us, certainly, but it also has a way of bringing to light some of the corners of our hearts that maybe have barely been—or have never been—seen before. It makes us actually crazy. Not cinematic crazy, where you throw something and then someone comes and holds you and you cry and then you kiss and then it's tomorrow and you're making breakfast and they're like, "You okay?" and you soft smile and say something like, "Yeah, I'm good." And then it cuts to the 4th of July at a friend's dreamy lake house.

I honestly don't have time for that kind of nonsense. Here's what I mean by crazy...

Have you ever dropped an AC unit out of your second-story window onto the asphalt below while some junior-high boys watched with mouths wide open from the sidewalk, because you were trying to move it alone, because you were so sad that you just had to do something productive to avoid your pain, and it almost pulled you out the window to severe injury if not death?

Have you ever burned your toast and then you were so UP TO HERE with life already that you punched your toast over and over again into the countertop?

Have you ever bought ice cream that was the favorite flavor of your college friend who died, to remember her, and every time you had a dinner guest and they chose mint chocolate chip, you explained that now this dessert was in her memory?

Yeah. That's more of what I'm talking about.

Grief is sad and weird and a little funny from time to time, isn't it? It's like a blanket that covers us. Sometimes it's suffocating, other times it's comforting, and occasionally it's somewhere in between. But these sorts of realizations are only possible if we're willing to pay attention to the grief in our lives and see it with grace filling the gaps. Like when I sit in the counseling office, listening to the gentle reminder of my therapist, I have learned to not just let myself grieve but also not be overly critical and pull it apart. Sometimes, we're just angry, and it will do more harm to add shame to the emotion than saying, "Yes, I am angry that this happened, and Jesus is still here, ready to love me through it."

Something in us loves to play the avoidance game so that we don't have to feel those hard emotions to begin with, right? We make excuses or numb ourselves with distractions so that we don't have to admit where we're at.

As it stands, we are living in a broken sort of world that carries all kinds of tensions around how we can hold joy and pain and marriage and funerals in our small hearts. It's never just one thing, is it? It's always a mish-mash of flavors, not unlike Rachel Green's trifle in that Thanksgiving episode of *Friends*.

And that's part of what drew me to Orchard House. It's a place that somehow stands in the past and present at the same moment—it carries a whole lot of history and narrative in its beams and foundation. I find so much comfort in this 350-year-old house. Maybe it's that it has stood for so long. I mean, the minuteman who lived there during Paul Revere's ride in 1775 watched the troops marching along and went out to join the ranks. But still, something being old is nothing special here in Massachusetts. My hunch is that it has to do with its defining narrative of this famously sad story. One that we cannot help but remember when we climb the stairs and gather in the study.

When I ask people on tour, "What do you think happened in this room?" they almost always guess that someone died there. Visitors from around the globe are poised for death. They're ready to hear the sad news. Not because they're all cynics, but they're comfortable talking about death because Louisa went first by telling the story of her own loss in the story of Beth. She was willing to put into writing the tremendous grief that everyone felt deeply.

It's amazing what can happen when someone goes first, friend.

***

Even after all of these months of grief, I still have moments when I really am not interested in going first. But then, I look around, and I realize that no one seems to want to hang with and actually invest in their grief. The only ones who do are the ones that can't seem to escape it. And we have a long history of trying to escape it.

Of course, we want to avoid death. I'd rather talk about happiness and success than what was said in a graveside service or how it felt when 21 shots were fired as my grandmother held the folded flag on her lap.

But as much as we'd like to skirt around it, we have to face that it's everywhere because, it turns out, every loss is a death. You may not be avoiding thinking about the passing of a friend. It could be the loss of a job or a hobby or a home or a season or a place. It could be the loss of a relationship or a past version of yourself that you liked more than the one you've changed into. But every single thing that makes today not the best day is linked to dying in some way.

We, as Christians, are people of the resurrection. We have this incredible hope beyond the grave, and yet we somehow are still afraid of the grave. Even though we sing and proclaim that death has lost its grip on us, we are keeping one eye on the exit in case death walks into the room. We talk tough about pain and suffering from our high-up towers, unwilling to descend to the earth below. To the dust beneath our feet.

Everything was cruelly unraveling and, eventually, it seemed to just turn to dust. I went from knowing who I was and where I belonged and what I "brought to the table" to being someone who fell asleep on the couch because going to bed felt like too much effort. I started to slip, and for months I slowly slid down the side of a hill into that valley of the shadow. This wasn't one or two losses. This was countless rejections and failures.

And all of this was tolerable at first because I kept telling myself that it would get better. But you can only do that for so long. You can only stand in the garden for a little while before you just start sobbing, wondering where Jesus is.

Sometimes, we use "hope" to numb us to the pain that's happening. We use the future as something we can anchor on in times of trouble or loss. And while that is a good practice—the kingdom of God is coming—it sometimes can make us believe the lie that our faith is a future faith only. That if things feel broken today, they'll get better tomorrow!

The truth is this: if the gospel—which literally means "good news"—isn't going to meet us in the pit, it isn't truly good news. If the doctrine you're believing isn't able to meet you where you are, it's out of focus. Maybe it's time we take a minute and figure out what on earth we've been preaching to ourselves all of these years. Because I can tell you right now that if everything gets ripped out of your hands and your Savior can't get to you, that wasn't Jesus you were hoping in.

So I'll take a page from Louisa's book, and I'll go first.

I'll tell you what I know because it's all I have left to tell you. When I moved to New England, I would have said that things were about to get started. That it was time for a new chapter.

Little did I know that these years would cost me everything. But somehow, it gave birth to the strangest and simplest and maybe most life-changing Truth of all: when we have nothing left to offer, we can receive his love the most. When we come with no ribbons or bows or whistles or tricks or good jokes, we can get down to the unfiltered truth that God doesn't want us to be the best, he just wants us to be his.

CHAPTER 2

The Chaos and the Fight and the Fog

I was tired, and we never make clear decisions when we're tired. Reaching into a box full of old hard drives, my fingers sifted through them, looking for a power cord to match. It needed a special adapter, and in a rush I grabbed the wrong one. I figured it would be quicker to choose one that was similar, but I knew it wasn't the one I was looking for. The drive started up with a little whir, but the speed was too high, and suddenly there was a pop, followed by a bit of smoke. I'd fried it and was left holding the cold metal in shock.

Panicked, I tried to get it to work again with another cable, but it was too late. I started crying, immediately feeling foolish about crying over a piece of technology. But it was more than that. It was videos and photos and memories from my college years. It held snippets of dates and dancing, and, as a film major, I always had a camera out and kept thousands of moments on this hard drive.

Sure, people 100 years ago were thankful to have just one image of a loved one. But when I sit here on a cold night, thinking of Jill and I meeting in college, I grieve the loss of that hard drive, which was probably filled with us laughing and telling stories and getting dressed up for the Junior-Senior

Banquet. So many simple scenes that I'd recorded suddenly felt like the most tender and important ones.

And that is what grief can sometimes be. I'm sitting here, trying to remember, but I can't give you file numbers and timestamps because grief just isn't linear or able to be cataloged like that. It's a vapor—or a puff of smoke from a broken hard drive—impossible to wrap your hands around, let alone your tired mind.

I wanted to control my memories and perfect their details all over again. I longed to have memories other than the strongest ones, which are the most painful. Memories that don't feel so heavy and allow for a clearer picture of our whole relationship. So perhaps this chapter is an exercise in making myself remember the times before her diagnosis. Trying to push through the initial brush toward a clearing in the woods. To find a place where we were sure we'd grow old together as obnoxious old ladies.

Somewhere in a box in my bedroom is a little envelope that's more narrow than wide. And inside of it is a bumper-sticker-sized card she'd made me that said, "Hell yeah, I want you to be my bridesmaid." I remember getting it and laughing because of her chutzpah. That was Jill at her core—all in and sure of what she wanted.

She was real and honest and always found the punch line.

I accepted her invitation to stand by her, but I'll be honest, I was not expecting it. I knew we were close, but in college, a whole lot of people can feel close. My friend Sandra once described it as living like puppies with everyone on top of each other, and that's exactly how it felt. We were always getting cupcakes or studying in each other's dorm rooms, and when I look for us in the back of my memory, we were just puppies borrowing each others' clothes and trying to grow up and finish our papers and fall in love.

WHAT CANNOT BE LOST

I'd had plenty of friends that I considered to be some of my nearest and dearest that never asked me to be in their wedding. Honestly, I didn't consider myself to be stellar bridesmaid material. In my own insecurity, I didn't presume that she trusted me so deeply.

Growing up, all of my best friends moved away, so having a wedding-level friend was a surprise. I'd been the maid of honor in my sister's wedding, but I was 17 so most of the load was carried by her friends who knew about bachelorette parties and how to show up on time for the rehearsal. I could barely drive, let alone give sex advice.

Jill and I stayed in touch about the details of the wedding. Late summer, small-town Minnesota, where her groom, Dan, had grown up. The bridesmaids wore yellow dresses because it was 2014, and I bought one from J-Crew that I never ended up using. Instead, on the day of the wedding, Jill pulled one out that belonged to her. It was more form-fitting than mine but I do have to admit that I looked good. Jill always knew how to help a sister find her fashion. I relied on her for that in a lot of ways.

She was a designer by heart and by vocation, so her wedding was pinterest-y in all the best ways. She had a plan of hanging tulle from tall pine trees, so we stayed safely on the ground while brave groomsmen climbed up to drape it. We became pros at tying burlap in bows. We had mason jars and went into a field by the side of the road to grab wildflowers, and I was both documentarian and friend, taking random photos and videos all the time.

The weekend was a blur, but it was a gift to witness her walking down the aisle to marry a good man who cherished her well. Dan was a true midwesterner in that he brought hospitality and work ethic to things. He knew that he had a good woman in Jill, and their union was one I was glad to promise to protect. On the plane back home, I wrote in my journal, "Jill is in good hands."

It felt like the whole future was in front of Jill and Dan until it wasn't. They were full of youth and promise, ready to take on whatever came their way. We didn't think—even for a second—that Jill wouldn't survive her 20s.

All we knew in those days was that she was a stellar dancer and always up for a good laugh and almost never sided with pessimism. She had vision and joy and, well, life.

We never saw the end coming.

Of course, we almost never do. We imagine longevity and don't dwell much on how life might end when it's just getting started. We assume we'll figure it out later. It reminds me of Naomi in the book of Ruth. She's married to a man named Elimelech, and one year, a famine no one saw coming hits; and they are forced to move. So he takes his wife and two sons to the neighboring nation of Moab. They're looking to start again, and his sons get married to women named Orpah and Ruth. It would seem that this family is thriving. But then, in just a space of three verses, all of the men die. We don't know what happened or how it all went down, but we know that they were fairly young because they'd been married no more than ten years.

I think of Naomi and the absolutely gutting loss of her men. Back then, the son would provide for his widow mother, but what happens when the sons die, too? With Ruth in tow, Naomi heads back home, uncertain of what is coming. But she does know this: all is lost.

In Ruth 1:19-21, it says:

> "So the two of them went on until they came to Bethlehem. And when they came to Bethlehem, the whole town was stirred because of them. And the women said, 'Is this Naomi?' She said to them, 'Do not call me Naomi; call me Mara, for the Almighty has dealt very bitterly with me. I went away full, and the LORD has brought me back empty.

Why call me Naomi, when the LORD *has testified against me and the Almighty has brought calamity upon me?'"*

This woman, who was just flourishing a few verses earlier, is suddenly the victim of famine. She knows what she had, and she knows what she has lost, and it seems she will never recover.

It's that feeling you get after a long cry, where you curl up and breathe heavy, out of breath from the agony. Your chest is pressed into the mattress from the weight of existing in that space. Face sore and eyes tired, you have nothing left. I am sure that on the days when her baby boys were born, Naomi never would have imagined that they would go first. I am sure that she believed that they would bury her, not the other way around.

Scripture is brimming with hurting people. And a powerful thing about this story is that there's not a rush to be better. Naomi was hurting for a long time and no one gave her a pep talk and helped her suddenly perk up.

So often in grief, our first instinct is to make it all better, but the reality is that we can't. There is nothing that we can do to quickly erase or undo the damage that has been done. Even if you stole a sucker from a baby and gave it back right away, there would be a loss of trust. If you said something unkind and immediately apologized, you've taken steps away from one another, losing intimacy. So Naomi is hurting, and the last thing she needs is someone to blindly preach to her about how everything will turn out for the best. They're not the ones sleeping alone and missing the babies they birthed.

Let me say this now: this story is just going to get messier before it gets lighter, and even then, the light doesn't undo the weight instantaneously. We have to wade into deep rivers if we want to get to the other side. We have to mourn what we've lost in order to find what cannot be lost. We have to acknowledge it and honor it in some way. Jesus isn't looking for you to get it all figured it out so that he will be impressed. He's asking you to get real and honest so that he can walk with you through the middle of the chaos and the fight and the fog.

Jill got sick at the new year. It's a story we've all heard about someone else. I remember seeing her post about it on social media, and it felt so casual. She had pain; it was a tumor; they removed it. She started a lighthearted blog called "The 1% Woman" about the process, but after only two posts, we were seemingly in the clear. The crisis was over and she was on the way to recovery. We made plans to go to Disneyland when her energy returned, and it was as good as set in stone for my next visit to California.

We started checking in more because we'd fallen out of the habit of regular communication and the scare left me longing to be closer to her. I felt guilty that by the time she was undergoing treatment and surgery and we knew what was happening, she was practically on the other side. She was eating well and keeping an eye on her health and went on vacation with her family. She was posting photos, and we were all exhaling, but there was still more to come.

It was the start of a new season for our friendship, but we'd been friends who could pick up where we left off because we'd been cemented together in our junior year of college by the most unlikely of experiences: bedbugs.

See, we were on different floors in the same dorm building in the heart of downtown Chicago. I was up on the tenth floor and she was on the fourth. One day, my neighbors got bedbugs and they started spreading. It was gross and terrible, and I came home one afternoon to my roommate putting all of her belongings in plastic bags. Our room had been compromised, so my roommate moved back home, since she was from the city, and I moved onto the fourth floor, where there was a single room up for grabs. The girls were new to me, and I didn't feel like making new friends, but Jill was there and this was our chance to dig deeper.

Things went simply enough. I had a little single room and she was down the hall with our friend Koral. We would study together and go to the movies and hang out in the lounge. I was a temporary resident, but they took me in like I'd always been there. After the headache of bedbugs, things were, it turns out, turning out ok.

Winter in Chicago was fully settled in, and the days got dark earlier and earlier. One afternoon, there was an officer-involved shooting on the street corner outside my window during a meeting I was attending. It sounded like a car backfired, but the pops kept happening and a man was critically wounded. I remember looking down on him, watching from a few floors up, unable to look away. It was the first time I'd seen a stranger in a fight for their life, and I knew it was sinking into my bones. I wanted to move past it, but it followed me. I remember thinking, "If you keep watching this, you won't be able to unsee it." And I was right. Over a decade later, I can see his face as he was covered with a blanket and loaded into an ambulance.

Down on the street level, people were gathered, and when someone overheard me telling another student I'd been there when it happened, it caught the attention of a nearby detective. He approached me, asking, "Did you see what happened?"

"No, I just heard it and then saw the aftermath" I replied.

"Well," he said as he pulled the police tape up above my head, "maybe this will jog your memory." He motioned for me to come with him. It was something out of a movie.

I didn't know I had a choice; I was in shock. I still feel the cold of an overcast Chicago evening. He asked me questions about what I saw and when he realized I didn't have some of the intel he wanted, he said, "Listen. I need information. An officer has been shot, and a man is dead."

It was the first time I heard that the man had died. The last time I saw him, he was bleeding through a blanket on a stretcher, being taken off to a hospital to make a full recovery. We finished our conversation, and when I crossed back to the other side of the police tape, I was met with news crews and reporters. I don't even know what I said, but my parents called from California to tell me that they had seen me on the news.

I wandered to the dining hall and felt a fog around me, but I didn't know what it was. My dear friend Jess asked if I was ok because she noticed the blank expression on my face, and I assured her I was. But then, someone dropped a plate on the tile floor in the serving area, and it shattered. When I heard it, I burst into tears. I didn't know I had post-traumatic stress, but my body did. And that was only the beginning of a semester of struggle.

One afternoon, when it was soaking in just how deeply trauma had already dug a barb into my mind, I walked down the hall to the room at the end on the left.

Jill was there and I lay down on her roommate's bed and Jill gave me a tissue while I cried. I was about to go through the hardest season of my faith life so far in the weeks and months that followed. I started having panic attacks and going to counseling regularly, trying to process through what had happened. At the same time, I also started changing the way I interacted with Scripture and theology, cherishing what I knew to be true. It was that messy combination of growth and grief all at once.

At times when my faith began to falter, I would literally sleep next to my Bible when I couldn't muster the strength to open it. I took God at his word when he promises to meet us and knew that even if I couldn't be the Christian I wanted to be, with a robust quiet time and all kinds of spiritual insight, he was near. And Jill was there, as a gospel-focused companion, to offer her kindness and friendship. She stood by me as I worked through the shock of death and now I see how that was almost foreshadowing.

Jill having cancer felt for me like sliding on ice. You slam on the breaks and start to slow down, only to realize that a collision is inevitable. She had surgery, and we were going to be ok. And then, the brakes locked up and skidded us further than was safe.

About six months after we thought things were in the clear, the pain came back and she could hardly move. She went to the hospital and over the next few days, we found out cancer was everywhere. Her liver, her lungs, her abdomen. While we had thought she was healing, it turns out the cancer was spreading. I cannot tell you how much I want to use swear words right now, but this is a Christian book and I'm not supposed to do that. But let me say this: it was swear-worthy.

I'd been pacing after getting that fateful text in which she'd asked me to pray, wondering what was going on, waiting for an update as they got tests and stayed in the hospital. I was back in California, visiting my family, feeling closer to Jill who was in San Diego, but still very far away. My nephew was going to be born any minute, and we were ready to rush to the hospital to welcome him. When we weren't painting my brother's new house ahead of the baby's arrival, we were chasing after my nieces and keeping trains on the tracks.

I wanted to be present in these beautiful moments, but when I think back to those few weeks, a lot of what comes up was checking my phone constantly for updates from the hospital. I wanted nothing more than to get in the car and drive six hours to Jill, but she told me to wait until they knew more. We were hoping that all was still well. But underneath the exterior of relative calm, I was on edge. One night, I shouted at my parents about something so trivial and stormed off to my childhood bedroom like I was a teenager only to emerge with an apology and tears as I said to my dad, "I'm just so worried about my friend."

And then, one night, she sent me a text and asked if we could have a call.

I couldn't get back to her fast enough. I stepped out onto my parents' front porch and sat on the top step, taking a deep breath before calling her. There was an anticipation because I didn't know what to expect. What do you say to someone who just got really bad news? Can I ask how bad it is? What does she need to hear? How do I find out what's going on without asking what's going on? Should I be upset or just play it like cancer is the most casual thing in the world and I'm not alarmed?

I hit the green button to call her and she answered.

"Hey," she said.

"How are you?"

"Not great."

We thought we were safe, but it kept coming.

Jill and I had places, I'm sure. We shared meals and adventures around Chicago, but when I think of her final months, our "place" is on the phone. My memories are in the car and on my parents' porch, and in my living room and walking around my small town, and she was there, but only in voice. I can still hear her trying to laugh but stopping because a coughing attack had started. She apologized and said she'd call back. I sat in silence while she tried to push through and regain composure, but when she caught her breath again, she'd often be too tired to continue.

I just sat there, listening to her worn-out voice tell me about the tests they were running and how absolutely exhausted she was. Endless exams and not a lot of clarity were wearing on her. When I asked her how to pray, she said, "Pray that I wake up in the morning." I felt gutted, and my body started bracing for the impact of God knows what.

I had been meditating on Psalm 3 that month. When I pulled it apart in Hebrew, I discovered that the literal translation is talking about how the enemies of the writer, David, were telling him that there was no hope. And then, to contrast their mockery, David writes:

"But you, Lord, are a shield about me,
my glory, and the lifter of my head." (v 3)

There's this proclamation that God is in direct opposition to those who tell David to stop hoping. God is the rebuttal to their calls and chants and suggestions that he should abandon any expectation of deliverance from his trouble.

And as David turns his heart away from their voices, he refocuses.

But you are the Lord.

Then he paints this beautiful picture of God as a shield—a protector from everything he is up against and the lies of his foes. He is "my glory and the lifter of my head."

No matter what glory lies before us or what accolades we could try and claim, whatever weighty honor is bestowed on us, our ultimate glory is God. Which means that in the greatest victory, he is the one that is better. And when we are downcast and discouraged—when we hang our head in absolute shame and heartache—God is the one there, too. The one who lifts our heads toward him.

In all moments, God is the best of the best and comforts us when things are the worst of the worst. God is the Alpha and Omega, the Beginning and the End (Revelation 1:8; 21:6), and here we see that he is also our victorious King and intimate comforter in times of dissolution and despair.

***

The next morning, Jill texted that she was still alive.

I returned to Psalm 3 and read these words again, but this time I noticed the verses that came around them:

"O LORD, how many are my foes!
  Many are rising against me;
many are saying of my soul,
  'There is no salvation for him in God.'
"But you, O LORD, are a shield about me,
  my glory, and the lifter of my head.
I cried aloud to the LORD,
  and he answered me from his holy hill.
"I lay down and slept;
  I woke again, for the LORD sustained me." (v 1-5)

She had woken up again. The Lord had sustained her. It felt like a miracle. But still, things were touch and go. We used to pray to make rent or for a good boyfriend or a decent grade on a paper, but suddenly we were praying for survival. Jill and I had intense but needed phone calls as September rolled on. I stopped asking how she felt, knowing it wasn't good. We held out hope for a miracle and begged Jesus to take it all away. We didn't want to plan for a funeral because we were young and she had been the healthiest person I knew.

One night, I sat in the car with her and we ran through the different scenarios. There were treatments to try and prayers to be prayed. Her church hosted a 24-hour prayer vigil, begging for a breakthrough in hour-long shifts. We were ready to go to war, but a quiet war was raging in each of us. Do I assume a miracle is coming? Or do I ask Jesus to bring her home? And what do I say to her? Every conversation felt like walking in fog, trying to carry on a conversation while wearing noise-canceling headphones, totally overwhelmed and not at all prepared. But we were out there in that unfamiliar territory whether we were ready or not.

Revisiting this story feels like the moment that the detective pulled the tape up, ushering me to come closer.

It feels like forcing myself to return to the scene of the crime. But in some strange way, it's forcing me to return to the scene of a miracle. The miracle that I got bedbugs and we shared a kitchen and grew close enough to travel and visit and stand together while she and Dan promised to be one until death.

I recently sifted through another hard drive and found the files of that warm wedding day in the woods. I clicked through images and saw Jill walking down the aisle in a video that I got someone to shoot with my camera. I heard the music playing as she gracefully made her way toward us in her flowing white dress as we all waited to meet her.

Jill handed her bouquet to her sister Emily. We all turned toward the front where she and Dan stood, ready to make vows "till death do they part." I heard a song by Sara Groves playing as the words rang out: "All I have needed, his hand will provide, he's always been faithful to me."

And I wondered, as I watched that day unfold all over again: he would be faithful here, too, right? He would provide in this mess, too, wouldn't he?

CHAPTER 3

The Glory Is at the Ground Level

Jill and I truly became friends over laundry. I walked in one night and she was there, folding laundry that she'd taken out of the dryer. It's always the worst when you don't make it to the laundry room in time and find your clothes in a heap on the center table. Someone else needed the dryer space and now, you have paid the price: wrinkled clothes.

But Jill was considerate. So not only had she pulled out the clothing; she was folding it, too. Honestly, a friend after my own heart. I remember standing there and talking to her. I can see it now: us standing in the later hours, she in her glasses, me in my workout clothes. I remember clearly that we made the connection that we'd met before but hadn't officially made an effort to get to know one another. She had a lanyard with her keys and student ID on it, which was red with the USMC logo on it because her brother was in the Marines.

There are very few friendships that I remember the start of, but, by God's grace, Jill's was one. I wish we'd known that we had limited time. I think back to the other places where we'd stand together just as we had stood folding laundry. Like me taking photos of her and Dan in their first apartment, or us dancing in the parking lot of a random bar for her bachelorette party, or in her dorm room after the shooting. We would stand together for a handful of years, never knowing until the very end that it was all so very temporary.

For a long time, I felt guilty that I didn't make every effort to spend every possible moment I could with her. There were missed calls and we canceled dinners and rescheduled movie nights because we had work or an exam the next day or a paper to finish. We were college kids making college choices.

I remember one night in particular just a few years ago when I had gone through a break-up and needed support. It was almost midnight in Nashville, but I knew that the West Coast was still awake so I called Jill in San Diego. She answered and I burst into my angry and distraught and insecure monologue. She listened and hmm'd and hawed until I was done and then she simply reminded me of what was true. She told me what we knew, even when I wasn't feeling it. And then, she quietly said, "Can I tell you a secret?"

I was certain it'd be life-changing news. Maybe they were moving or expecting a child or had won the lottery! My mind raced for a moment as I prepared myself for all of the excitement in the world.

"What is it?" I asked.

"Dan and I are thinking of getting a dog."

Even now, I sit and smile at her overhyping of a normal moment. No fireworks for parades here. Just a woman thinking about maybe getting a dog. We didn't take classes or go to conferences about how to build a friendship; we just existed together in the kingdom of God.

For the record, they did get a dog. A corgi, no less. His name is Darryl, and when I finally met him at Jill's memorial service, I held onto him with equal parts joy and sadness.

We griped about work. We kvetched about boys. We rolled our eyes and bought dinner on Sunday nights because the dining hall was closed. We lived ordinary lives and never knew to pay them close attention and cherish them.

Still, there's a part of us that values the cinematic over the true to life, no matter how much we try to be down to earth. I got my first taste of that when I was about eight years old and went to a big Christian event with my family. It was a Billy Graham crusade in Oakland, California. An all-star lineup of DC Talk, Jars of Clay and Michael W. Smith led the music and Billy Graham preached. When he asked people to come forward and give their lives to Jesus, I found myself disappointed that I'd already made that choice. I mean, how cool would it be to accept Christ at a Billy Graham crusade? Even though my experience of meeting Jesus was just as meaningful, it was the first time I wished that I'd had a more epic "coming to faith" moment. A few years earlier, after hearing the story of Jesus at a Vacation Bible School, I'd found myself in my childhood home, sitting on the carpet and asking Jesus to be my friend and Savior[1]. No fanfare or cheering. I also remember that day because I learned how to snap my fingers, which is another major milestone for a kid. But when I watched the masses come forward at that big Billy Graham event, my own story felt massively underwhelming.

This is nothing new. I remember other times when the idea of a thrilling moment was so desirable that I felt pressure to perform, and I'm not the only one. I stood with a few dozen people on the banks of the Jordan River as a young adult and watched people get baptized, and noticed that a few of them had already been baptized but felt that being submerged in the Jordan was a better testimony of their faith.

We express the wish that we had a "more dramatic" testimony or a more captivating story to tell. We believe lies and think, "I don't have anything to say about the Bible

---

1 You can read more about what, or rather who, my faith is in, and why, in the Afterword on page 143.

because I didn't go to seminary." We assume that only the put-together or educated people get to lead. And whether or not we realize it, we prove that ordinary isn't particularly appealing to us every time we perk up when hype kicks down the door and runs into the room with a tee-shirt gun.

We say that we want to ask Jesus into the simple and quiet moments, but we keep turning up the volume.

Why is it that we just can't settle for a normal life?

We're always looking for the glimmer of glamor. For the hint of something beyond us. This is nothing new—we see it constantly in our own ache for filters and photoshop. We are a save-face culture, and that particular mindset can go all the way back to the garden, but I'll stop the rewind this time in the Old Testament book of 1 Samuel.

The people of God have been rebelling and trying to go their own way for a long time. Before King David or any other king reigns in Israel, the prophet Samuel is in charge of the people's well-being. He's the spiritual leader of the Israelites and one day they take a look around and realize that all the other nations have kings and they're discontent with not having a man on the throne to say the least.

This has to be incredibly discouraging for Samuel, who goes to God and relays the message. Kindly, he's told by God,

> *"Listen to all that the people are saying to you; it is not you*
> *they have rejected, but they have rejected me as their king.*
> *As they have done from the day I brought them up out of*
> *Egypt until this day, forsaking me and serving other gods,*
> *so they are doing to you. Now listen to them, but warn*
> *them solemnly and let them know what the king who will*
> *reign over them will claim as his rights." (1 Samuel 8:7-9)*

God wants us to know that his way is best, but he's not going to hit us over the head with it. In fact, many times before, God had given a warning shot, saying, *Are you sure you want to do*

It was October and I was speaking at a church in New York, so I had to drive about four hours to the city. I'd decided to stay with my friend Rachel in Connecticut. Rachel and her husband are both cancer survivors, and so we were talking about how things had been, and I shared that it felt so uncertain and we were taking it one moment at time. Suddenly, Jill texted that she needed to talk. I stepped into a side room and listened as she asked for prayer and told me how things had been. We talked about fear and not knowing and prayed together for endurance. I told her to call me if she needed anything because my phone was set to always ring for her.

That night, I went to bed but woke up around 4am to Jill's number lighting up my screen. I picked up, and she was in tears, not wanting to worry anyone but needing prayer because she couldn't breathe. As a woman who had ventured through the shooting and other traumas, I knew panic when I heard it and started in on coping mechanisms.

Our bodies don't always know how to find peace. The panic button gets hit, and it releases stress hormones into our system, and our bodies go into auto-pilot. We stop being rational, and we shift into survival mode. Like that night when the plate hit the dining room floor and I burst into tears, it's entirely involuntary. There's no rhyme or reason when we're looking to calm down and we can't.

My friend Natalie walked through cancer a few years ago, and we talked about that experience recently. She was honest and it was a reminder to me of what happens when we're so very weary—when our bodies are under pressure for such a long time.

As she shared, I was reminded that when someone sick is overwhelmed, it is not an absence of bravery but the presence of a threat that they cannot control.

People like to use heroic language with those who have terminal illnesses. We say that the person is "fighting cancer" and when they die we say that they "lost the fight." We make them soldiers, as if they signed up for the draft. Other friends of mine who have faced cancer say the same things and it bears repeating: they are not warriors—they are weary.

And this is the truth about someone having cancer or a terminal illness: whatever their disposition, God's grace is enough for them. They don't need to muster courage or grace for a fight and it's completely unfair to put that kind of pressure on them. They do not owe anyone any kind of performance. If Jill had been angry and never picked up the phone and cut us all off, that would have made perfect sense. Because death just doesn't make sense and there's not a way to get there perfectly.

Jill's whole body was under threat and she was strong and kind and faithful. Her whole body was being attacked and she was thoughtful and wise and hopeful. Her whole body was experiencing what many of us will not and I will tell you until my voice goes hoarse that she was, by God's grace, exactly enough, entirely herself and fully loved.

During that middle-of-the-night call, I remember getting right down to business with her. Asking her to breathe with me. Letting her know it would end and that the fear wasn't forever. We prayed for peace and comfort and slow, steady breaths. We prayed for the miracle of calm in the storm. We begged Jesus for another morning. And this is maybe what has always stuck with me: Jill loved Jesus even when—especially when—things were darkest.

Eventually, we fell asleep, and the next day we talked on the phone for hours as I drove the rest of the way to New York. We talked about random things and told stories, and it was just one of those calls with an old friend where suddenly so much time has passed. Sometimes she had to hang up and call back so she could rest or catch her breath, but this new sort of surviving-normal was a pattern that we both seemed to settle into. The weariness and the pivoting and the hour-by-hour and the gallows humor became common place.

I returned to Massachusetts, and we continued on from day to day. We never again had long, meandering conversations or the stamina for much more than short bursts. We never again talked about boy problems or what movie to watch or how much we loved a certain song. Things slowly quieted down, but somehow that made them seem more chaotic.

***

"January, 1858.—Lizzie much worse; Dr. G. says there is no hope. A hard thing to hear; but if she is only to suffer, I pray she may go soon. She was glad to know she was to "get well," as she called it, and we tried to bear it bravely for her sake ... Sad, quiet days in her room, and strange nights keeping up the fire and watching the dear little shadow try to wile away the long sleepless hours without troubling me. She sews, reads, sings softly, and lies looking at the fire,—so sweet and patient and so worn, my heart is broken to see the change."

In late 1857, the Alcotts had decided to move back to Concord to be close to their friends. Lizzie was still struggling, and they tried what they could to revive her health. Louisa took her to the sea to see if that would help things. They found doctors in Boston to attend to her—a debt that Louisa paid off for years. Needing a place to settle down, they bought Orchard House, the ultimate fixer-upper.

Though it would be months before they actually moved in, the family spent their time building and wallpapering and making it their home. Lizzie couldn't do a whole lot, but she provided plenty of lightheartedness where she could. She didn't feel well, but she was always her kind and intentional self.

*"February.—Dear Betty is slipping away, and every hour
is too precious to waste … Lizzie makes little things, and
drops them out of windows to the school-children, smiling
to see their surprise … Dear little saint! I shall be better all
my life for these sad hours with you."*

***

At the end of October, I found myself on a plane to North
Carolina for a weekend with my friend and mentor, Lisa.
She is the real deal and invited me to spend a few days doing
absolutely nothing epic. We sat on the couch and took naps
and ate comfort food and got lost in the Brushy Mountains.

There is a gift in a friend who is willing to let you come
and rest with them. We didn't spend our days doing the most
exciting or interesting things, but we spent them doing the
most vital work of friendship: existing together and looking
for Jesus in all of it. I cannot tell you how much of a ministry
it was to me to have a friend so present and so thoughtful and
who fed me carbs so well. Lisa sistered me and mothered me
and bossed me a little, and I will always be better for it.

One afternoon, while Lisa and I were in the car, I got a call
from Dan. He had Jill with him, but she wasn't able to talk.
We had a brief conversation and prayer before I said to her
something that is now forever in my memory.

"Jill, I need you to feel better so that we can go to
Disneyland," I said with a sad smile on my face.

There was silence for a moment, and then Dan replied,
"She says, 'I'll get right on that.'"

What I didn't know then was that this was my last phone
call with Jill. There was no great speech or tearful goodbye
or even a realization of the weight of that moment. Just two
friends making plans that would never happen. Sometimes,

we feel unsatisfied when words exchanged don't feel like the right ones, as if every ending must be underscored.

My friend Jamie was a senior my freshman year of college and on the morning she graduated, we were supposed to have one last hang out but I overslept and was so upset because I felt like we didn't get that final meal together, and she kindly looked at me and said, "Melis, our friendship speaks for itself."

That grace was what I've tried to carry with me for all of these years, though I drop it much more often than I'd like to admit. But I keep hearing Jamie's encouragement when I want to live in shame or try to force a bow on top of moments that are ordinary and simple.

I think about Jill promising to "get right on that" or Lizzie dropping gifts out the window to those below, and they blur into one. I sit here with a computer, typing away, and it feels like Louisa could be upstairs in my guest room switching the pen from her left to her right hand, pouring out what she has as a way of processing things. We're all trying to make some sense of the senseless, right?

Louisa called her time of losing Lizzie "sad days and strange nights," and as time went on, I, too, found myself waking in the middle of the night not only from the nightmares I had but from overall anxiety, wandering between the hours, unsure of what was next. I was sleep deprived and frozen all at once, living what felt like a ghost life. I was there, but I wasn't truly present. And this is what grief does to us—it pulls us away from ourselves, and we no longer feel like we know who we are or what we're supposed to be doing.

I woke up in the mornings with adrenaline coursing through my bloodstream as I checked my phone for any kind of update, and slowly, that became more familiar to me than anything else. My journal entries from that time talk a lot about not remembering what it felt like to be fully at ease, or to feel safe. About how this new reality was no longer the exception but the rule.

Sad days and strange nights are what land us in the valley of the shadow. We are so used to surviving that we take one step at a time and then look up to find that we're in a wasteland, and nothing seems to be familiar. But the funny thing is, on the outside, the fall of 2019 was straightforward. People who didn't know me too well saw me serving at church and giving tours of Orchard House and applying for marketing jobs while finding freelance gigs to stay afloat. But inside, something was chipping away at me with every bit of hope deferred or every update in which we weren't seeing improvement. A constant stream of small losses left me in a space where my only companions were empty hands and head-shaking disbelief.

In Mark 5, there's a story of a woman who was bleeding for twelve years. Scripture says she "had suffered much under many physicians, and had spent all that she had, and was no better but rather grew worse" (v 26).

Anyone with a chronic, or long-term, illness knows the horrible cycle of getting your hopes up for healing over and over again only to be let down. There was no reason why she should have held out hope any longer. But she heard that Jesus was around and how he could heal and she had to see it for herself.

There was a crowd around him, and it was basically going to be impossible for her to have an audience with him. Given the fact that she had been bleeding for so long, she was culturally considered impure. So, as an outcast, it was even more of a risk to show up where others were present. But desperate times called for desperate measures.

She reached out as he passed by, and suddenly, she felt in her body that she was well. There's one important thing to note here: she touched the hem of his garment. Now, while

WHAT CANNOT BE LOST

that might seem like a rather uninteresting fact, there was a history behind it.

Back then, an inheritance was often accompanied with the giving of a robe. It signified that the person wearing it would be the one to inherit the birthright. In Genesis 37, a man named Joseph received his father's robe. Only Joseph shouldn't have gotten it, because he was the second youngest son—nowhere near the eldest. So his father wasn't just buying him a nice jacket; he was handing him the last will and testament. He was leaving his possessions and blessings to one of his youngest sons. It's no wonder Joseph's brothers were fuming mad—he had been given the greatest gift his father could have afforded.

So when the woman who is bleeding touches Jesus' outer coat and she is healed, there is this poetic moment in which she inherits healing from the Son of God. His legacy is one of wellness and true shalom—that is, peace, well-being, and wholeness. But even more amazingly, Jesus notices this woman. He stops and calls her, inviting her to a personal encounter with himself. And the powerful truth is this: Jesus himself is our inheritance, not just what he can give us. He is the gift.

The woman is now healed, but before she can sneak away to rejoice in anonymity, Jesus stops dead in his tracks and asks, "Who touched me?" (v 31)

The disciples think he has to be kidding. Everyone is touching him! This is a super-crowded area. But what he's getting at is that someone has touched him and it matters. All-knowing as Jesus is, he turns and we are told that the woman is trembling. She is fully vulnerable after years of being an outcast; she has spent more time away from people than with them.

She was trying to fly under the radar after over a decade of living in the shadows and outskirts, and now all eyes are on her.

Verse 33 says, "But the woman, knowing what had happened to her, came in fear and trembling and fell down before him and told him the whole truth." Her response to the shock of encountering Jesus was to tell the whole truth. She had no choice but to come undone before him, not out of terror but out of awe. Because for so long she'd been silenced and struggling, and now, she was free. Free to speak and to confess and to be received.

Jesus looks at her—as everyone watches to see how he will interact with this woman who, because of Levitical law, shouldn't even be allowed in this public setting—and he says, "Daughter, your faith has made you well; go in peace, and be healed of your disease" (Mark 5:34).

I wish I could tell you I lived as an inheritor of healing during those days. I wish I could tell you that I felt the safety and nearness of Jesus as I wandered through those sad hours of watching and waiting. I wish I could say I started every day with long sessions of Bible study and worship and total faith in whatever Jesus was going to do. But the truth—which I have the freedom to tell—is that I went to a dark place that I had nearly no choice but to go. It's hard to endure long seasons of suffering without some dark moments.

Louisa thought she knew grief. I thought then that I knew what it felt like to lose. But the truth was, we were both walking a different trail. One that would lead to the Valley of Shadow. Rather than a year of thriving, we would bleed and it would be longer than we'd imagined before full healing actually happened.

CHAPTER 5

Eternity's Shore

Every part of our stories is something caught between poetry and passing comments. One moment, the sun is rising and the birds are welcoming a new day as the breeze floats across the marshes. The next, you drop the almost-ready avocado you found at the grocery store and lament that it's probably ruined. (Spoiler alert: you just paid almost two dollars for a ruined avocado.)

Jill's death both was senseless and made sense. Everything about it was a constant juxtaposition, and it threatened to pull my heart in two.

When a story stops at death, it feels like trying to button your coat or tie your shoes with numb fingers. You're grasping for what you know is there, but somehow you just can't seem to get a hold of it. There's a reason ghosts in stories we read as children show up and leave with no real logic. They mysteriously make themselves known on their own time and in their own way, leaving the haunted to shout into the darkness.

Hello?

Don't leave.

Come back.

The story I'm about to tell you feels like it needs a thousand caveats, but it's probably best that I just write what happened. I can't tell you a lot of details about the weeks leading up to November 22, but I can tell you that it had been raining for a very long time. Late autumn storms in New England cut through with whipping winds and dark clouds that somehow made the marshes brighter. The green beachgrass of the summer shifts to bright orange and then a tired rust color. It's probably the richest of the fall colors because it'll stick all the way through the winter.

When I moved to Massachusetts, I made it a point to live near the coast so I could put on my duck boots and make my way out to the marshland, which floods and dries up hour by hour. My friend Ed says that the Great Marsh is always different and doesn't change, and he is right. One local historian wrote in the early 1900s, "There are also reasons for believing that as the land sinks, the Marsh, soft and uncertain as it seems, is really more stable than the everlasting hills."[2]

During low tide, my favorite hiking path is dry enough to walk along. I had discovered it accidentally, just before the summer. A construction project meant another trail had to be moved, and this seemed like a good shortcut. It wanders through woods on the Crane Estate, a historic site on the coast surrounded by pristine dunes, woodland, and beachfront. A massive Gatsby-esque estate house sits on the top of the hill, looking over it all, reminding us of a heyday long passed.

When I think of those final days with Jill, I often think of how I couldn't lay my eyes on her but I heard her over the phone. It is a strange thing to use your hearing to process the reality of losing a beloved friend. I don't have to try hard at all even now to recall her voice in it's weariness. I cannot imagine what it's like for those of you who are or have been

---

2 Charles Wendell Townsend, *Sand Dunes and Salt Marshes*, 1913, p 209.

constant caregivers in the room as your loved one is in pain. I wish that I could sit down with each of you and hear your story about how loss has shaped and scarred you, and give you words of comfort, but I also know that when we're in grief, we're in shock, and words never really seem to make up for what we've lost.

Though the memory is laced with an ache, my mind still cherishes that text I would get from her to talk when she was needing an outside voice to tell her the truth. Over the previous months, we'd built a new sort of liturgy of conversation. I would know she was exhausted and she would express her needs in straightforward ways. And tell me that she needed an anchor in something eternal. Not trite sayings or empty promises or prosaic hopes.

"Hey," I would say.

"Hi."

"You want me to just pray?"

"Yeah."

I don't know what I prayed for, but it never felt like the right thing to pray for. Do you pray for relief? Do you pray for endurance? Nothing seemed very clear, and after I said "Amen," Jill would ask me to talk to her. After a while, I got into the habit of simply recounting the story of the Bible. "Well," I started, "I don't know what to say. And I don't know what is best. So let's go back to what we know is true. In the beginning, God created the heavens and the earth."

We talked about creation and the fall and all the ways that God had acted. All the ways his people abandoned him. All the stories we already knew. We'd met in Bible college, for crying out loud, but when it came time to cry out loud, all that came out was the parting of the Red Sea and the fact that Jesus walked on water. When we're caught in the middle of the most severe of storms, it turns out that him walking on the water toward those whom he loves still happens even today. I didn't know if it ever helped her, but I just kept repeating the narrative of Scripture over and over like my life depended on it—and Jill's too.

November arrived, and soon, Jill had been gravely sick for longer than expected. Part of the normal rhythm of my days was checking in, sitting in silence, and more recently getting occasional updates from her husband. I'd stopped texting Jill a few weeks before when she got too weak to respond.

In some ways, I never had the chance to say goodbye to her. We had been surviving each day, and the last thing I wanted to do was admit that my fears were all coming true. She was strong and weak all at once, and I knew that my job as her friend and confidante was to listen and pray and encourage her. Death wasn't at her doorstep; he was in the room, and she knew it.

We all did as time went on.

Jill started hospice, and the pacing continued in my living room and around the apartment. Every morning, I would reach over to my phone and check for the bad news. I would let out a sigh of relief because she was still alive. And then I would feel my muscles tighten because I knew she wasn't going to last much longer.

One afternoon, in between tours, I sat in the guide room when one of the guides, Anne, started reading Louisa's journal out loud. She was remarking how much money Louisa had made and how successful she was, and I found myself drawn to the book in her hands because it had never occurred to me to read Louisa's retelling of her life. It felt too personal and private to read someone's diary without their expressed permission. But every morning, I'd been opening my own worn-in journal and spilling out my heart, and I was just looking for some words to nod along to.

So I picked up a copy from the shelf and made my way to the hallway outside of Louisa's bedroom. I sat there, in a chair by the attic door, reading about how Lizzie was getting sick again and how the Alcotts were fluctuating between hope and despair. About how she had a good day here and a bad day there. About how, when Lizzie seemed to be improving, they would all "hope a little."

> *"November, 1858: I lead two lives. One seems gay with plays, etc, the other very sad—in Betty's [Lizzie's] room. For though she wishes us to act, and loves to see us get ready, the shadow is there, and Mother and I see it."*

Facing death, even from across the country and over the phone, feels like a constant loss, even before the final breath. So I'd walk the halls and point to the Alcott's belongings, telling stories and answering questions. I'd fiddle with my name tag, telling the people about Beth, ignoring the deep weight of having my own Beth in the back of my mind and the forefront of my heart constantly.

***

And Louisa was right: death eventually moves us into a double life, out of survival more than anything else. On one hand, the dishes have to get done and there are parties to attend and babies to photograph, and on the other hand, Jill's own shadow was appearing, just like Lizzie's. I was trying in some ways to pretend that my life wasn't actually happening and hers wasn't actually ending.

One stormy week in late November saw day after day of rain, but it finally was letting up, so I texted my friend Bea and asked her to go with me to the Crane Estate. We bundled up and I grabbed my camera—the first desire to be creative in weeks—and we took to the trail that led to the marshes.

The grass was a golden brown from getting wet so late in the season. It lined the sandy trail that our boots carried us along.

And here's the thing about the beachgrass: it's an environment maker. It traps and keeps little organisms that stay in the marsh and help it to thrive. Its whole task is to keep things in place so they don't drift out to sea during high tide.

The wind was hitting in gusts and the sky was darkening long before sunset because of the heavy cloud cover. I caught a glimpse of it as we neared the end of the trail that led to sand dunes and then shoreline: a break in the clouds. It was a thin, golden line where the sky was opening up and the sun was so low that it caught fire in the strangest way I'd ever seen.

With every step, I was in awe as the sun ducked under a shelf of cumulonimbus and reflected upward, its light stretching across the clouds. It turned the world a strange glow of pinks and oranges in a way that had Bea and I enthralled. We pushed our bodies against the insane winds, working our way along the coastline back toward the estate as the sun turned the beach an otherworldly series of colors. I pulled out my camera, capturing every little bit of it that I could, and I turned to Bea and said, "I feel joy. I haven't felt joy in a long, long time."

Have you ever felt that shift between two emotions that feel at odds? Like when you're so very angry, and then the person you're mad at makes a joke, and you get a little softer around the edges. Or when you're sniffling, and the friend you're crying to says something like "He wasn't that great, anyway." And you have to let out a little laugh.

Sometimes you feel these unpredictable and confusing emotions, and it's also mixed with a bit of self-interrogation. How dare you feel a positive emotion during a devastating time. My friend Taylor Leonhardt wrote a song about how we're like mountains that encounter bad weather and keep standing and our feelings are like the passing storms. We're not the weather or the wind, but the mountain that stays. And if you're carrying these complex emotions, you are not the only one. Your body needs to pause from sadness sometimes, and that's not a reflection of how little you are committed to lamenting and honoring your loved one.

My body was exhaling after months of waiting and wondering, even if for just a few minutes. For a moment, it was as if Jill wasn't sick and struggling, and I wasn't tied to my phone waiting for heartbreak. In fact, the marshes are one of the only places where I don't have cell service. For a moment, the world was a thin place, connecting heaven and earth, with God's glory seen in clouds and sea and sunset. Every streak of bright pink and orange that my eyes witnessed filled up my heart and I smiled in disbelief.

We hiked back through the woods to the estate house and it took nearly an hour, but we made it as the night took over, our steps getting more and more precarious as the vesper light gave way to the evening. I threw on the only song that felt appropriate for such a strangely light and peaceful reprieve: "Live Forever" by Drew Holcomb and the Neighbors. The chorus swelled into "I want you to live forever underneath the sky so blue," and my wrist felt the familiar vibration of a notification on my watch.

I quickly glanced down and saw two words from Dan: "She's Home."

Death, even when you see it coming, always catches us by surprise. We have to sit down and remember to breathe and take in what is happening in our disbelief. We are never truly ready for the end and the void and the exhale that never inhales again.

I reached over to Bea and grabbed her hand and said, "Oh my God. Jill just died."

***

"March 14 1858: My dear Beth [Lizzie] died at three this morning, after two years of patient pain. Last week she put her work away, saying the needle was 'too heavy,' and having given us her few possessions, made ready for the parting in her own simple, quiet way. For two days she suffered much, begging for ether, though its effect was gone. Tuesday she lay in Father's arms, and called us round her, smiling contentedly as she said, "All here!" I think she bid us good-by then, as she held our hands and kissed us tenderly.

"Saturday she slept, and at midnight became unconscious, quietly breathing her life away till three; then, with one last look of the beautiful eyes, she was gone … So the first break comes, and I know what death means,—a liberator for her, a teacher for us."

I read those words sitting by the attic door that day when I'd decided to pick up Louisa's journal. I looked up, watching the sunlight in her room. It landed on her bed, where a quilt lay folded up. The pattern is a series of triangles made to look like flying geese. Lizzie was a quilter and seamstress in her free time because it required very little physical effort from her sickly frame. We know that Marmee made that quilt, but it would make sense to assume that at some point, Lizzie's hands were on it too.

In the book and the movies, the attic is the space where the March sisters play and dream. In reality, it's used for storage, barely insulated, and full of cobwebs. It doesn't feel warm, but it's a place in which to take a break from the rest of the house. On winter afternoons when I need to find quiet after guiding, or even as I've been editing this book you hold in your hands, I go to the attic. It's no surprise that Louisa portrayed it as a place of escape.

I sat in the peaceful space of the landing of the second floor of the house, imagining Louisa slowly pulling that quilt off the foot of the bed and wrapping it around herself, walking past me, and opening the door to the attic to find some space to grieve and process. I imagined her pacing like I'd been doing in those final weeks of Jill's life. And for a moment, I could see her there, almost making eye contact with me as I held her journal 150 years later, giving me a look as if to say, "I know."

I think of my friend Clarissa, who has the gift and curse of knowing loss, and of how she has been able to come alongside me. As grievers, it is so vital that we build friendships that allow us to be in the company with those who have mourned with Christian hope. It gives us a pathway to follow that leads to the foot of the cross and allows us to bring a friend along for the trip, even though our experiences are entirely different. There is a familiarity that brings comfort and understanding in a way that we so need. When someone else has seen or heard or walked out what you have, it sometimes puts language to what you haven't had words for.

A month before it was released, we were given the opportunity as Orchard House staff to see Greta Gerwig's *Little Women*. As we all stood in the hall outside the theater, we were buzzing with excitement and almost nervousness as we waited to be seated. When we made our way into the room where we'd view it, we settled into our places and quieted as the words emerged onto the screen:

> "'I have had lots of troubles, so I write jolly tales.'—Louisa May Alcott"

It was a delight to finally see this beloved story on the big screen, and everything was so hopeful until it cut to a gray day on the beach. Beth was sick, and Jo sat with her, reading stories to distract her from her illness. Beth sat up and told Jo that she wasn't afraid to die, and immediately I felt my heart start to unravel. The two actresses were telling the story of my loss and the location that Gerwig had chosen for that scene was the Crane Estate.

Even now, years after losing Jill, I go back to the trail at the Crane Estate, and whatever my demeanor, I suddenly start to feel lightheaded when I get to the pathway near the dunes. I flash back to that sunset of wonder and hope and joy and the shock of loss, and my body knows before my mind does. I've learned to take deeper breaths and push through. It seems that the beachgrass managed to trap all of my memories of November 22. There is an entire ecosystem of my own complex grief that is embedded into the shorelines and marshes.

During the movie, Jo and I both sat in disbelief at Beth's words: "It's like the tide. It goes out slowly, but it cannot be stopped."

"I'll stop it," says Jo as she leans over and puts her head into Beth's lap. Beth embraces her, and then, without even knowing I was going anywhere, I was back in my room weeks earlier, softly saying to Jill, "In the beginning, God created the heavens and the earth."

Part of me understood, but most of me didn't know that when I was telling Jill Bible stories, I was growing up into someone different. At some point, I stopped telling her my own woes of job searching and writer's block and the new sweater I got, and just went back to the basics of Scripture.

We wandered from Genesis and creation to Exodus and God setting his people free.

We moved from the sun standing still to the walls falling down to the time that Naomi thought all was lost.

We trekked across the desert seasons and the rebellions and the countless times that God called his people back through prophets and priests and kings.

We remembered how people wanted a savior and one night in the little town of Bethlehem, he showed up in the most unexpected way. And then, he brought good news and laid down his life for those he loved and conquered death and spoke so very kindly to a weeping Mary in the garden.

It seemed that my trivial experiences just didn't carry enough weight for her deathbed. I know that we often believe that the Bible is too boring or too strange to understand, but here's the thing about the truth: it always ends up being what sticks.

I've heard stories of people singing hymns in their final moments or family members reading Scripture to their loved ones. Jill died with worship music on in the background. Something in our souls is bridged when we remember the gospel to the very end—especially at the very end.

Listening to her move slowly toward Jesus, I got a glimpse of what it means to walk faithfully to the finish. I hope that when my time comes, the thing I request of my loved ones is that they tell the Old Story that has been repeated for generations. I hope that I memorize God's words and can repeat them even if one day my memory goes before my body does. I pray that I hide his word in my heart in a way so that it always steadies me, even if my hands start to shake and my steps are uncertain.

So when I feel my grip starting to loosen or my steps start to slide on the ice of disbelief, I go back to afternoons on the floor of my bedroom, sitting beside my dresser. I go back to Jill's hoarse request for me to talk and remind her of the truth. I go back to the beginning and it makes more sense of how her life ended. It's the beachgrass that holds everything together and keeps us from floating out to sea during high tide.

CHAPTER 6

Lifting Up
Our Arms

Traditional church calendars are broken into seasons that have names and traditions and rhythms, like keeping step in a repeating dance. Jill died at the very end of the second period of Ordinary Time in liturgical church calendars. Other church seasons include Pentecost, Lent and Advent. You may have heard of some of them, but I'm here to tell you that Ordinary Time feels the most like home to me because I'm not always feeling like the other seasons, but this one is for anyone anywhere.

Some parts of the year are intentionally heavy and others celebratory, but Ordinary Time is a bit of both. It holds the tension of normal life and is meant to remind us of how our faith is one that is ordinary, too. These days feel so simple with no holidays on the horizon, but I find that Christ meets me in Ordinary Time in special ways.

There aren't candles being lit or special songs about Christmas, but I get to look for truth in daily life. For example, when I open Scripture to find Jesus providing food for his people, a sandwich takes on new meaning. When I read about him setting people free from their trauma and sin, I walk out of counseling a little lighter. When I read about how the heavens and earth proclaim his glory, a drive through the farmland at dusk takes on a different, worshipful tone. He is always working and always displaying his majesty in some way, and during Ordinary Time, I sense it with fresh eyes.

As details came together for the memorial service, I started looking into plane tickets, and another kind of grief showed up: the ways that not having a job was taking its toll. At that point, I'd been without work for four months, and every single penny went into absolute necessity.

I want to be the writer who can tell you about the ways in which I was strong or brave and skip over the uneasy and more vulnerable parts, but I realize that the fact of the matter is that I'm limping alongside most of the people who read my words. I avoid payments right up until they're due out of fear that I won't have enough, and that season of joblessness broke a lot of things in me. I try to fight a scarcity mentality, but in a world of things and dollars and uncertainty, it is easy to try and secure everything that I can.

At first, the challenge was not knowing what to say to people when they asked me what I do. So much of our conversation is based on this identified and shared experience, and suddenly, I was empty-handed and unable to feel impressive in any way. I couldn't hide behind an organization or mission statement or any kind of status symbol. While other friends were buying homes and going on vacations, I found myself struggling month after month to make ends meet. And the worst part was that I was going all-in on job interviews.

I didn't just send my résumé to companies; I wrote personalized cover letters and designed whole landing pages complete with welcome videos and branding that matched the colors and fonts of the jobs I was applying for. I reached out to anyone who might know of an opening and I cannot tell you how much of a failure I felt like when so many rabbit trails became dead ends. I figured out how to make it on about 25 dollars a week for all of my meals and tried to make it seem like all was well, even though my mind was constantly racing around how much I was losing. At any given moment I could tell you exactly what was in my bank account.

After a while, I couldn't say, "I am in between jobs," because it'd been so long and I was afraid someone would figure out that no one wanted me. And that's maybe the hardest pill to swallow after you're let go. All of the experience and drive and résumé-building doesn't guarantee a quick solution to unemployment. While the lights were staying on and I was eating the same three meals for months on end, there was this massive lack that I couldn't avoid.

So when I sat there, searching for flights across the country for Jill's memorial service, I felt trapped. It was paralyzing because the service would be three days after Thanksgiving, and all of America was traveling so prices were the highest they could possibly be. I went online, and I looked and looked and felt my body and heart go completely numb.

I put the task to the back of my mind for a moment and before I could gather the courage to try again, a friend texted me and asked if I'd gotten my ticket yet. I told her no, and she told me that she was going to take care of it. Her exact words were "Ok buddy—let's get you a flight."

Sometimes when we are grieving, it feels like spinning wheels in mud. There's no clear way forward, and reversing seems foolish, and you're left moving quickly and simultaneously going absolutely nowhere. What you need is for someone to put on their boots and walk up to your car and knock on your window and try to lend a hand. You need someone to show you that there's a world outside of these spinning wheels. That's what this beloved friend did for me. She watched with everyone else for a moment and then said to me, "Ok. That's enough. I'm here, and we're together."

I'm sure you've had someone walk through a season of want and not known what to say to them, so I'd like to spell it out for you: put on your dang boots and go to them. Maybe it's making a meal or offering a plane ticket. Maybe it's going on a walk or caring for their children. Whatever it is, it will be helpful because when we're beyond exhausted, everything is effort. Every hour and errand and to-do is soaked in a weighty ache. Sometimes, when we've been hurting for a long time, it's as if our muscles get so fatigued that we can barely lift our own hands.

In Exodus 17, the people of Israel were facing their first battle after being freed from the Egyptians and a life of slavery. It was against Amalek, their staunch enemy. They had made it this far only with the help of God, so their leader Moses carried a staff which represented God's power. This staff had appeared before when it turned into a snake as he stood before Pharaoh. And he had held it in his hands as he encountered the burning bush before that.

The people of Israel were hardly organized at this point. And they were certainly outnumbered. They were a new nation who had been raised in slavery, and they did not have much to offer, but they did have the sovereign power of God with them.

> "Whenever Moses held up his hand, Israel prevailed, and whenever he lowered his hand, Amalek prevailed."
>
> (Exodus 17:11)

As long as he held up that staff—that reminder of who they belonged to—the Israelites won the battle. But his arms got tired because he was a human person with limits.

The story continues:

> "But Moses' hands grew weary, so they took a stone and put it under him and he sat on it, while Aaron and Ur held up his hands, one on one side, and the other on the other side. So his hands were steady until the going down of the sun." (v 12)

This idea of steadiness can also be translated as strength or faithfulness. His hands were shaky and worn out, but they needed strength to faithfully do this thing. And he took it as far as he could, but the truth is that he was an ordinary person and could only carry so much. And rather than saying, "Oh, God will provide" and moving on, his companions and fellow soldiers knew that sometimes, the Lord provides by giving us the gift of one another.

So they showed up and they held his arms, and this was how the battle is won.

In those dark days after Jill died, I didn't have a whole lot to offer. I started the day with some semblance of focus, but by the afternoon, I was a mess and barely knew what to do with myself, let alone how to work out logistics for a cross-country trip. I needed backup. It reminds me of that passage of Scripture that describes how the church is like a body made up of many parts:

"For the body does not consist of one member but of many ... But as it is, God arranged the members in the body, each one of them, as he chose. If all were a single member, where would the body be? As it is, there are many parts, yet one body." (1 Corinthians 12:14, 18-20)

I was like a twisted ankle in need of some reinforcements. I could sort of get around, but it was only going to get worse if I didn't have someone step in for support.

One night, my friend Brooke texted, "I'm sorry this autumn has been grief on grief."

She offered her husband's coordination skills to me, and I told her I was thankful but didn't want him to call me because I was a mess, crying on my couch. The next thing I knew, she was at my door with food options and ice cream. Her husband Jon had remembered from months earlier that my favorite flavor—brown butter almond brittle from

Jeni's—was at Whole Foods. She sat with me and let me be sad and helped me come up with a game plan.

I think often of the gift of companionship in that moment. I remember that my friend Grace covered a rental car so I wouldn't have to worry about that, either. They all knew that I was struggling financially but never made a big deal of it. They just said, "I'm taking care of this."

They held my arms up.

Jill died a few days before Thanksgiving, and I was with my friends Tim and Ann for the holiday. We were up in Maine, and everyone was celebrating the beauty and the snowfall, and I was in a fog. Nothing felt totally right, but I was able to be with people I loved and not alone, which was a mercy. The morning before the memorial service, I got on a flight that was covered, and then I rented a car that was covered, and stayed in a hotel that was covered.

I spoke briefly at Jill's memorial service and saw friends I hadn't seen in years. We gathered together to remember and share stories and catch up, and I kept feeling like Jill would be there in a matter of moments. It felt unfair for us to gather without her. I kept looking to the hallway, waiting for her to come out and join us.

A woman I didn't know walked up to me and said, "I think it's so sweet that you gave the speech at her wedding and her funeral." I had totally forgotten that I'd spoken at the wedding. As I stood there and thought about it, it felt so backward and strange. There's nothing fine about the fact that I'd watched her walk down the aisle and listened to her die within a decade.

When we were gathered together after the service, Jill's sister Emily brought me into another room and gave me the dress I'd worn in her wedding. Carrying it around was bitter, but sweet. A reminder of a dear friend as we all remembered her, without her in the room.

I stayed with a childhood friend, Amy, that night, and my flight got canceled on the way back to Boston, and it afforded me a chance to grab brunch with my friend Grace. We sat, and I probably cried, and we heard a rumor that our friend Vivian was nearby so we went and found her in a local coffee shop. We shared apple slices and reminisced, and for a split second, the world felt normal even though my body was in shock from stress and lack of sleep. I flew back through Chicago and stayed with my college roommate, having dinner with our friend and again, I felt a wave of oasis in the midst of wasteland.

Life is supposed to have a pattern. It's supposed to follow a path that feels predictable. We fall in love, we commit to others, we have children, we raise them, we get promotions, we retire, we live well, and then we die when our bodies give out from old age. We say that we don't like a cookie-cutter life, but I would beg to differ. Because every time that we start to see the story go sideways, we protest. Every time a perceived injustice happens or a job is lost or a life is cut short, we are full of confusion and hurt and anger. And underneath anger, there's almost always a deluge of sadness when we slow down enough.

The unspoken truth here is that we are desperate for Jesus to keep us right in the middle. Not too close to failure, thanks. Not too close to loss, thanks. Not too close to any kind of chaos, thanks.

But that's simply not how this story goes.

This story is one that veers into brokenheartedness before it gets any better.

One of the biggest lies that can deceive us in our faith is that we live in one space or another; we are either fine or a mess, grieving or joyful. There's not a ton of room for feeling a tug of war in our hearts, which is where we most often find ourselves.

We like clear storylines with a start-to-finish, not a mess in the middle.

But the days after a loss, and the weeks and the months, can be tricky and mean and unfair and unclear. And we desperately need help but don't know what to ask for.

Maybe you're there right now, or you're watching someone walking through this deep valley. Oh, friend, I wish I could sit down with you right now and tell you that it isn't fair and it isn't fine. It feels like your heart has been ripped out of your chest and there's nothing you can do to stop the bleeding. Like all of the light and laughter you once shared will never return and there's no reprieve on the horizon. Grief is blinding and deafening and paralyzing, all at once and yet, we have to keep stepping forward, which feels very unfair.

The world keeps spinning and the Kardashians keep buying things and new albums drop and films are released. It feels like you're the only one in these trenches, knee-deep in mud, fighting for your life.

This is when I take refuge in the word of God, when it says, "The LORD is near to the brokenhearted and saves the crushed in spirit" (Psalm 34:18).

***

The Alcotts couldn't afford a house. They could barely afford much of anything. After years of the family trying to make ends meet, it was the generosity of their friend Mr. Emerson that even made Orchard House a possibility.

He had the wealth they didn't, so he put a down payment on the property, but it needed a lot of work. Honestly, no one wanted this tired, old fixer upper. It was worn down, and so were they.

Louisa wrote in her journal that she was resolved to make money and provide some semblance of stability. She was sick and tired of moving place to place, uprooting and wandering. Her ache was for home.

Bronson had the help of his friends, and together they spent about a year making the house liveable. They connected the two buildings together, and when Bronson wasn't traveling for lectures or teaching his students, the Alcotts were wallpapering and making it their forever home. Lizzie was sick the entire time but she was there, too. In fact, she died just weeks before they moved in.

So when Louisa and her family made their way to Orchard House, they were a bit lost. They were reeling from the fact that she was gone, taken at only 22 years old.

Sweet Lizzie had to be laid to rest about a mile up the road on top of what would later be called Author's Ridge in Sleep Hollow Cemetery. Sometimes, I go to the hillside and see all the Alcotts there with small, unassuming headstones. Lizzie was the first to go, but almost all of them met her there eventually. I wonder what was going through her mind when she knew that she was dying. She seemed, by Louisa's account, to have made peace with leaving early. She even chose the place where she wanted to be buried. When I visit, there are often pennies left behind on the plot—a tradition that honors the dead. It started as a way to pay respect to veterans of war, but as time went on, they sometimes appeared on the graves of those whose battles weren't as literal.

The family deeply wanted Lizzie to be back with them bringing perspective and simplicity and thoughtfulness to the house. In a home built on loud debates and theatrical performances and big personalities, Lizzie was the slow, steady one. She brought the even pacing and tempo. Things felt somehow silenced without her quietness.

We still have her melodeon (a kind of small organ) in the dining room, just below the stairs that lead up to May's room.

We have strict rules in Orchard House about touching things because over 80 percent of what you see there really belonged to the family. We dust and clean things, but we do so with training and gloves and very specific instructions. The windows are made with a special UV blocking layer so that sun damage can't happen. Visitors aren't in a museum that holds pieces of art, but the house itself is the work of art. We protect it fiercely because we know what it represented to the family and how it has held so much meaning in the world for so long.

One afternoon a few months ago, I was standing near Lizzie's melodeon and I noticed that someone had left a penny on it. After the tour I put on gloves and carefully retrieved it, but it felt like the visitor that had left it understood the story of Lizzie (and Beth). This was not a random act. They understood that in her heart and her mind and her body a war was raging as she came to grips with death. She moved toward it with grace and honesty and fear and humanity, and that was something worth honoring.

That melodeon is silent now, but I imagine that it was something that brought so much life to the Alcotts, and there is something especially heartbreaking about a silenced instrument. To the untrained eye, a melodeon looks like a small piano, but it's more of an organ or accordion as it needs air to be pumped through it to make sound properly.

On a recent tour, a child was in the dining room, and when I turned around, I saw her little fingers on the keys, pushing one of them completely down. I stood there in momentary shock as she lingered in curiosity over the old instrument. Her mother immediately apologized, pulling her away and keeping a closer eye on things, but after it happened, the thing I kept thinking was "Why didn't it make a sound?" And then I remembered: it wasn't filled with the air it needed.

There was no true life in the keys so of course they produced silence. Stillness hung in the air, but what else would?

And that's what is so truly awful about death: it brings silence. We find ourselves met with nothing when we expect sound. We think they're going to call or text or send us a Christmas card. We assume they'll walk down the hallway or in the front door, but they never do. Or we experience the loss of certainty and no one reassures us; the loss of a job, and no one thinks to ask how it's going; the loss of a home when we move, and no one asks how we're settling into the new place.

This ache and void does a number on us, and Louisa felt herself being drained over the course of the coming months. Her older sister, Anna, got engaged to John Pratt, and May was pursuing her art lessons. Louisa had likely assumed that Lizzie would take care of their aging parents to some degree and she would be free to write and teach, but suddenly, the responsibility fell to her. This pressure built up over time, and she ended up in a dark place of despair.

This happens when we lose someone loved by a lot of us. The feeling of loss is so overwhelming that we feel stuck, unable to move forward without them. I think of my friend Clarissa, whose husband died suddenly in a hiking accident, and how she writes about her fears that she wouldn't be able to make it without him. She was paralyzed by this gaping hole in her life. Even if it's not a partner, but a close friend or family member, it's normal to feel weighed down into despair.

At one point, Louisa decided that life was too great a burden to bear, and she actually went to a bridge near Boston, determined to end it.

There are gaps in her journals around this time because she burned so many pages later on as a way of protecting her privacy, but she does tell about the shift in her temperament.

> *"October: Went to Boston on my usual hunt for*
> *employment, as I am not needed at home and seem to be*
> *the only bread-winner just now ... My fit of despair was*
> *soon over, for it seemed so cowardly to run away before the*
> *battle was over, I couldn't do it. So I said firmly, 'There is*

*work for me, and I'll have it.' And went home resolved to
take Fate by the throat and shake a living out of her."*

***

About a month after Jill died, I went on a hike in my hometown
with a friend, and it was going to lead to the most splendid view
of the surrounding area. There was rain, which was giving way
to fog, and as we climbed the switchbacks, we started to wander
right into a low cloud. As we got closer and closer to the top, I
found myself getting disoriented because instead of seeing the
view after a 2,500-foot elevation gain, I was seeing only total
white. There was no sense of distance, and I had to stare at my
feet as we neared the summit because my depth perception was
so severely affected. I felt a small panic rising up in me and
had to force myself to take deep breaths to keep from getting
more light-headed as we made our way down the narrow gravel
paths.

It felt appropriate to those first few months to be hiking
into a fog. Even as I attempted to gain some perspective, I
was caught again in the haze of grief and couldn't seem to
get away from it. While I never despaired of life itself the
way Louisa did, I certainly had moments in which I felt that
losing this dear friend was something so jarring that I might
never recover.

And this is another challenge of moving forward after we've
lost someone we deeply love: we never get over it. I remember
reading about how our friends bring something out in us
that only they can. I remember so clearly the songs Jill and I
would sing in the dorms and the jokes we made with effortless
humor. It was something that only she brought to life in me,
and when Jill died, it felt like that part of me died with her.
I don't use the same tone with other friends, and I don't call
them for the same reasons I called her. We don't just lose our
loved one when they die; we lose part of ourselves.

Which is why we so deeply need someone to remind us of what is true. In the early days of grief, we're in a fog and we need friends who will not just walk with us or lift our arms, but will carry us at times. We need meals brought and ice cream delivered, but we also need someone to remind us of the truth of who we are and what we are here to do.

And I suppose this is also where the church calendar comes in. Because Jill died at the end of Ordinary Time, but her memorial service was on the day Advent began. Advent literally means "waiting," and it's not about the pomp and circumstance and singing and jolliness that we often confuse it with. Rather, it's about longing and praying things like "O Come, O Come, Emmanuel."

On the first day of Advent—the day of the memorial service—my church back at home lit the first candle of Advent: the candle of hope. They sang about Christ's coming and in some way believed for me that it was possible to look forward to tomorrow. I was standing by a lake in California, remembering my friend, in a black dress that she would have loved, holding her dog that we'd long awaited, so very far from home.

But the people who would carry me through the coming year were together, gathered, singing of the coming hope and beginning Advent on my behalf. And that's the mystery that we call the church. We are one body, even when separated by miles and seasons and circumstance.

The candle of hope is meant to signal the beginning of the watching and waiting that Advent brings. We are longing and lamenting, eager for the relief that Jesus alone can bring, but which will only fully arrive at his Second Coming (1 Thessalonians 4:16-17). We're just starting the journey of moving toward his arrival and the first thing we need is hope that it's even possible to believe he has come and he is coming again, but we need to make space that won't be made on its own. We have to take time to slow down and notice and allow our hearts to move at the pace of spiritual growth, which is often slower than we'd like.

As the weeks went on, things stayed unclear and foggy, but I knew that I wasn't entirely lost, and that made those early days feel more bearable. With each text and phone call and kind note, I still felt so alone, but as I settled in for winter, I knew one thing: hope wasn't gone. At least not yet.

CHAPTER 7

The Honest Truth

I've always felt a bit anxious on planes, but in recent years, it has become more challenging for me to be at peace when suddenly a shake or a drop shows up. In my 20s I crossed the country and occasionally the ocean, a whole lot, so much so that one year I traveled over 35,000 miles. You would think that I'd be a seasoned veteran and a jolt wouldn't take its toll on me—that after all of the plane crashes I'd never been in, statistics would bring me peace.

But the truth is this: after a loved one dies, statistics don't matter anymore. Jill was the 1% woman. She was the healthy, 28-year-old who got cancer so aggressive that doctors just called her unlucky because they couldn't explain it any other way. You can tell me that there's only a one in a million chance my plane is going down, but it doesn't matter to me anymore.

Everything is out of my control, and nothing is predictable. There is no "sure thing" in this world that can bring my soul to a place of peace and finding my way back to Jesus was a long and, at times, completely exhausting road. But it had to start with getting honest.

I couldn't even tell you where I was flying, but I can tell you I was going north. I was already tired and ready to be on the ground again when it started and I decided to just let go and write what was going on in my head.

> "*The plane hits turbulence, and I can't fight the panic anymore.*
> *I'm too deep in the grief now. I've stopped remembering the feeling of Good News on the other side of unexpected phone calls.*
> *I'm numb around any semblance of being thrilled about the days to come.*
> *And this is what grief is today: I'm in that place of standing on the shore, a downpour blinding my eyes.*
> *I have to take off my glasses because they're covered in rainwater, making my vision even worse. It's hard to breathe when the wind blows, and it's been dark for a while, but we're not at the breaking point that promises morning.*
> *I could go inside and try to dry off. Pretend the deluge isn't happening. Warm myself until I'm out of logs for the fireplace. But eventually, they're going to burn, and I'll have to come back out here to get more.*
> *I'll have to face this reality again.*
> *I just want to talk to her again.*
> *I would tell her now what I wouldn't tell her before: that I've been scared this whole time.*"

So much of the time that Jill was sick, I was afraid and felt the need to not be. To trust more and to hope harder and to not go there. I'd seen others lose themselves in the wasteland of their own losses, and I was certain my story would be different. I would find the silver lining. I would utter my hallelujah. I would lift my hands up and sing with a shout of praise. Isn't that what a Christian is supposed to do?

I would not be the person who let the darkness in, and wasn't Jesus going to be so proud of me for it? Wouldn't he reward me for my amazing faith and my steady endurance? I supposed that my sadness could be comforted, but my anger was probably a step too far. That was giving way to something that felt less measured and more intense. So I never said it until that moment months after her death: I had been scared the whole time.

I know that I am not the first person to try and impress God with my emotional discipline. We are out here trying to give him what we think he wants, but over and over again he makes it perfectly clear that what he desires from us is for us to stop trying to fake that we're on his level. We are not divine. His holiness literally means he is "other." He is set apart. And rather than making us feel that great chasm of distance, it's actually an invitation to let down our guard and remember that he decided to get on our level.

Jesus starts his ministry and gathers twelve disciples to stay close to and draw near. They travel together, and dine together and from the start, Jesus is very clear with them that there are things beyond what they can see in the immediate. Things that are a mystery but eternal and good. One day, this is what he says:

> "'A little while, and you will see me no longer; and again a little while, and you will see me.' So some of his disciples said to one another, 'What is this that he says to us, "A little while, and you will not see me, and again a little while, and you will see me"; and, "because I am going to the Father"?' So they were saying, 'What does he mean by "a little while"? We do not know what he is talking about.' Jesus knew that they wanted to ask him, so he said to them, 'Is this what you are asking yourselves, what I meant by saying, "A little while and you will not see me, and again a little while and you will see me"?'"
>
> (John 16:16-19)

We know now on this side of the story that he was talking about his own death and resurrection. But for those who hadn't lived that part of the story yet, what he was saying was confusing.

Jesus has this uncanny ability to be entirely relatable and straightforward and otherworldly at the same time. It seems that the disciples didn't always understand Jesus the first time, because they weren't looking at things the way he did, with eyes focused on an unseen kingdom.

This was nothing new. Jesus was almost always misunderstood or others forgot his track record. For example, his first miracle of turning water into wine proved his power. People started to get anxious that there was no wine at a wedding and Jesus was able to provide, and yet his ability to provide was continually questioned throughout his ministry. People forgot that he's God and started to panic when there was no food, until he was able to provide miraculously yet again.

We read these stories and roll our eyes at the disciples for lacking faith. Hasn't he done it before? Why wouldn't he do it again?

Perhaps one of qualities about Jesus that we find most unexpected is that he is consistent. We read in Hebrews that Jesus Christ is the same yesterday, today, and forever (13:8), but that is a concept that's tricky to grasp. We regularly assume he's going to abandon us or suddenly change his mind and decide we are not worth loving or caring for or comforting, but everything in Scripture points to the opposite reality. When he says that he will do something, it always comes to pass (Numbers 23:19). His yes is yes, and his no is no.

Yet, we forget to take him at his word—and forget that he is the Word; the first and the last and the only. Our human brains just do not compute the person of Jesus, but he is committed to proving himself over and over again so that our fickle human hearts might receive him.

The disciples still don't know what to make of his language and, rather than asking him for clarity, which he would gladly provide, they start to talk amongst themselves and assume things without going to the source. They start to implicitly question whether he is really for them and whether they are really safe—and he's fully aware of it because he is God. And as God, one of his attributes is omniscience—which means he is all-knowing.

So while the disciples think that their conversations are something he is not privy to, he is fully aware of their confusion, and in his kindness, steps in. Brené Brown says that clarity is kind, and I think that Jesus shows that kindness in offering them the relief of knowing.

And beyond that, I love this passage of Scripture because it points to the fact that Jesus is gently inviting them to come to him first. Not to go around and ask others in an attempt to understand, but to go to the source. In short, he wants their honesty. He wants them to show up without pretense or filters or without even figuring things out on their own first.

At the heart of his relationship with the disciples, Jesus is calling for honesty because he desires for them to walk in truth. We see the Holy Spirit called the "spirit of truth" several times in the Gospel of John and so, as Christians, one of our core values is truth. And that includes telling the whole truth about what we're wondering about and struggling with, and bringing those things to God.

If the disciples are showing up to conversations from what they think is a safe place that is distant and they're not entirely engaged, Jesus is getting a filtered version of them. I think that we've all been in situations where somebody was holding back on their commitment to something or even to us. Some of us have been in relationships where we were all in and the other party was playing some cards close to the vest, and it ended up in a painful conversation once all of that came into the light. And this is why vulnerability is so dang hard. It feels like exposing yourself to someone that might hurt you or respond in a way that breaks your heart.

While I think there is a place for wisdom and boundaries and holding things in a way that is protecting yourself in our relationships with each other, we can always come to Jesus knowing that he is completely safe and his actions are for our good. We can always show up fully with Christ, just as we are, because nothing is hidden from him anyway. I spent a lot of time during that year of loss trying to come to Jesus in better shape. Just one more lap around the track or a few more lunges or a couple more reps. I believed that I could always be faster, better, stronger spiritually, as if that's what Jesus wanted. As if he was keeping score. I never paused to think that maybe he would still meet me when I was winded and slow and tired. That he would meet me anywhere at all because he's everywhere all the time.

Listen to me when I say: Jesus is not the boyfriend who left you or the spouse who betrayed you or the boss who said you were doing a great job and then let you go. He is not the parent who walked out or was emotionally unavailable, he is not the friend who said one thing and did another, and he certainly has proven over and over again that he loves and delights in his people.

And yet, because we live in a world with all of these broken relationships, it's really hard to trust Jesus enough to be honest with him. So in some sense, I don't blame the disciples for the way that they were hesitant to ask Jesus for clarification. They were living among humans and had seen what mankind is capable of, so in an effort to look good in front of their leader, they tried to figure things out so they wouldn't seem incompetent or unprepared.

One of the reasons that we often hold back in our relationship with God is that we believe that he wants us to be not only competent but also put together in a way that is simply impossible. There is no way that someone can be completely knowledgeable about all things and completely confident all the time and completely in control for even a moment, let alone a series of moments.

But when I start to feel like Jesus is distant or unaware of my struggle in an intimate way, my mind wanders to the story of Lazarus in John 11. Famously, Lazarus was a friend of Jesus' who died, and Jesus brought him back to life. And Jesus, being God himself, knew that he was going to do this miracle, but we read that he wept when he saw Lazarus's sister Mary grieving for him. He wept because his heart broke over the heartbreak of others. And he knew that death was something worth mourning. He wept because he was closely acquainted with grief—a man of sorrows (Isaiah 53:3).

Another kind of sorrow is realizing that so much is out of your control. When Jill died, I felt that, and even now, as I try to think of things that are truly within my grasp, I can come up with very few examples. And that's because the world we live in is entirely outside of our jurisdiction. I can drive a friend to the airport, or I can take my car to the grocery store, but that doesn't mean that I am at all the one calling the shots on the road. Someone could sideswipe me or rear-end me or cut me off or make a decision that impacts everything for the rest of my life. And I say this not to catastrophize as much as to remind us that we are very human. But despite this, our impulses to control and to be seen in a certain light are very common. The disciples just want Jesus to think that they get it. But he knows better—he always does.

"Jesus knew that they wanted to ask him, so he said to them, 'Is this what you are asking yourselves, what I meant by saying, "A little while and you will not see me, and again a little while and you will see me"?'" (John 16:19)

He knew they wanted to ask them. It was as if he was just waiting for them to be honest so he could to say, *Ah, yes. There it is.*

***

My unraveling was not only witnessed by God but was received with compassion by him as well. I had a résumé of skills and education that I kept as a safety net, but one day that no longer seemed to matter. It was in losing that net that I realized how much I was used to trusting in it.

To tell you that things got difficult in that season feels like an understatement, as you would see if you were to scroll back through my social media. I can assure you that I was being honest, but I didn't preach much about how I knew amazing things with confidence unless they were eternal things. I didn't post about what I had but what was lost. I was trying to make sense of what was happening, but I truly didn't have much to show for it. My hands were empty, and not just for a moment but for over 15 months. Even now, a year later, I still feel shaky and stressed because of what that season brought to the surface.

I was desperate not only to be financially stable but to be stable in every sense of the word. I had been thrown off kilter, and then, in the early spring, the pandemic hit. I don't need to go into detail about that because all of us lived through it and continue to live through the aftereffects of it, but I can tell you this: when you've lost your job and you've lost your friend and you've lost many of the things that anchor you in life, whether you realize it or not, the final proverbial nail in the coffin of your confidence is found in spending weeks alone.

It was scary and it was strange and at first, I thought that it wouldn't be so bad, but as time went on, I realized that this was a whole new reckoning of the way in which I saw my dependence on Jesus. Suddenly, he was the only other person in the room. And that's when things get real.

We stood around the Orchard House gift shop restocking and talking about COVID-19, wondering if we would ever close the doors. After all, tours had been taking place for so long that in theory, someone could have taken a tour of the house, gone to Europe and boarded the *Titanic*. Hardly anything could close the house, so we assumed that nothing would. And then, that night, I was about to watch the Utah Jazz versus Oklahoma City Thunder game and they canceled it right before it got going. It felt so strange and I felt fear rise up in me for the first time. The pandemic made all of our pretending fall apart, especially in the quiet of our own homes and minds.

To try and find some normality in those early days of quarantine, a friend and I decided to spend mornings together via FaceTime reading the Book of Common Prayer. It has morning prayers and noon prayers and evening prayers that have been prayed for hundreds of years, and doing that seemed like a practice that could ground us a bit.

We would begin our calls by talking about the things that were stressing us out and how uncertain everything felt. Should we stay put? Should we travel to see family? Would that be jumping the gun too much because maybe all of this would be over in a matter of weeks? Would it be wise to wait things out? We spun our wheels over and over and over again in the mud of not knowing, and one morning, I woke up, and I was done.

I remember so clearly when we had that call for morning prayer and, in exasperation, I said to my friend, "I just feel like I've been trying to prove myself for so long, and I've been trying to push forward into job searching and staying so optimistic because of what it is that I have to offer professionally, but now I find myself asking what the point is. Because it feels a lot like my problems would go away if I just got another respectable job with a respectable income.

And that's part of the problem. Because if you told me that the whole reason I should get out of bed in the morning is so that I can have a cool job or do interesting things, I just don't think it's worth it anymore. I feel like I'm so beyond caring about social status, because it's been ripped out of my hands, that I'm simply not convinced that the best reason to get out of bed is to have something impressive or interesting to say at dinner parties."

When we walk through hard things, well-meaning friends often remark that it'll get better. Just keep your head up because, soon, everything will be ok. But as the months went on, those words didn't mean anything anymore. I had been in late stages of getting a dreamy job when COVID hit, and suddenly, they reached out and said they weren't hiring for a year. I was ready to move onward and upward, and suddenly I was sliding back into the valley again, saying, "Wait, what?" Everything that felt within my grasp was gone again. A vapor.

***

We might say that life is not about things or status, but try removing all of the things and any perceived status and see what happens. I think of the rich young man, who we read in Mark 10, approached Jesus and who had loads of accomplishments socially. He was challenged by Jesus to give away what he was hanging his identity on, and it says:

> *"Jesus, looking at him, loved him, and said to him, 'You lack one thing: go, sell all that you have and give to the poor, and you will have treasure in heaven; and come, follow me.' Disheartened by the saying, he went away sorrowful; for he had great possessions." (Mark 10:21-22)*

Just as the pandemic highlighted to all of us how dependent we are on community and face-to-face interactions, which we had to spend a lot of time avoiding, my season of grief reminded me that so much of what I had been chasing in searching for a stable job had become an idol. It wasn't just that I wanted to pay my bills; I wanted to prove that I was competent.

And finally, after job searching for six months, with all potential leads burning up with the onset of a pandemic that made everyone freeze their hiring, I could finally start to get honest with Jesus about how things really were.

I wish that I could tell you how Louisa responded immediately after and in the months that followed Lizzie's death. But the windows that we have into her life are very limited and fairly foggy. She was a survivor: an incredibly accomplished seamstress, she was not above cleaning the floors and doing household chores. She took whatever work she could find even if it wasn't glamorous.

Louisa was living in a time when the main goal was survival. There was a war breaking out, and the child-mortality rate was around 37 per cent. That meant that over one third of children wouldn't make it to their fifth birthday. No one was thinking about having it all—they were thinking about having anything at all.

In an effort to do work she believed in, Louisa became a nurse in the Civil War. She went to Washington, D.C. and helped in a hospital where she saw great losses and death and illness. She was strong and healthy and able to lend a hand, which was something she deeply wanted to do. Louisa had no shortage of conviction, and since she could not fight—which I am sure she would have loved to do—she played her part by bringing those who were ill and wounded back to health.

The days were terrifying, and the things she witnessed were heartbreaking. Men crying out for their mothers and drawing their last breaths. She wrote about her experience in her book, *Hospital Sketches*, and it deeply changed the way she saw the world. One day, her supervising nurse came down with something that they called "typhoid pneumonia." It didn't take long for Louisa to catch it, and suddenly, she was in a fight for her own life.

At first, she just stayed put, trying to ride it out. But as her health declined, it was time for her to get home. She made her way back to Concord, and when she arrived, her family were shocked at the sight of her. She was a ghost of the person she had been before, weakened and feverish. I wonder what it was like for her parents, who saw her lying in bed, struggling as Lizzie had done. She was hallucinating and barely conscious and the family prepared themselves for the worst all over again. For weeks, it was unclear if she would pull through.

Orchard House had just been recovering from the loss of one daughter and now they had to face that possibility again. Marmee cared for Louisa faithfully as she first lost her strength and then slowly regained it. There were dark nights and frightening moments, but eventually Louisa fought her way out of the clutches of death. Still, she had a long way to go and what the family didn't know then was that the medicine she had been given was Calomel, a medication full of mercury.

Louisa was no longer in danger of death, but her body had taken a hit that was far more than she could have imagined. She wrote about the struggle of pushing forward and lamented over all that she lost. From running daily to barely sitting up straight, she says, "I was never sick before the war and never well after it."

This is grief. The first major shock to our system wounds us, and we never fully recover. We don't look at things in the same way that we used to. Death was something we were never meant to know, but the second the clock started ticking, the moment that brokenness entered the world and each human life began to end, it became a character in a story we had to learn to live with.

Our wounding from loss marks us. Sometimes, we go about our day and feel as though all is "normal" and we have made a full recovery. But then, the wind gets too cold for our lungs or the angle of a step brings back that bad knee or a memory resurfaces and we're back in that stuffy room, praying that healing is possible. We're back to aching and missing lost things and even if it's a wave that lasts only a few breaths, it's enough to knock us over again.

We have to learn to live with our grief. We adjust things and make room for it. I keep a photo of Jill on my gallery wall in my living room, and it's more prominent than the one from her memorial service that I had for so long on my fridge. I carry her memory with me when I make a new friend or watch a goofy movie or talk to her sister who has the same voice she did. And these days, it doesn't cripple as much as it used to, but it still shapes things a bit.

When someone loses a loved one to cancer or a friend to illness or accident, I think of my beloved friend. When someone says that they're watching a parent or family member fade, or taking care of them in some way, I remember Louisa's words about her sister again:

"I shall be better all my life for these sad hours with you."

God's purpose in healing is not that we should just be the same as before. It's that continue with a new perspective that allows us to know the heart of our suffering Jesus. Just as he ached for the honesty of the disciples, he desires us to be honest with him. To come as we really are. To just look him in the eye and say what's in our hearts and minds.

I couldn't be loved more by God if I pretended I was well. In those solitary, isolating days and nights in my apartment, I couldn't front anymore. I had to admit that I was angry and hurt and lonely. I had, in many ways, come to the end of myself. Nothing left to show, nothing left to prove. Hundreds of prayers for someone to survive that weren't answered with a resounding and miraculous "Yes!"

I needed to be honest. I needed to get so very angry on that plane when everything was out of my control and I had no more resources to fake composure. After all, death is something worth being so very angry about.

One afternoon, my friend and pastor Bobby called to check in with me. He knew I was at my apartment slowly going mad, though I'm sure he didn't expect to find me at rock bottom. He asked me how it was going, and my response was "Well, you know, I have nothing that I contribute to the world and nothing to show for myself and I'm sad and I really don't think anyone misses me because I don't have a role to play that can't be replaced."

Bobby was taken aback by my blunt answer.

I was tired. I was done pretending that I wasn't. And as I sat there on my living room floor on the phone with Bobby, it was as if Jesus came around the corner, took a seat right beside me and said with kindness and maybe a slight smile, *Ah, yes. There it is.*

CHAPTER 8

Empty Hands

Part of the aftermath of grief is the realization that you've fallen behind tremendously. Which lends itself to anger or frustration. It's up to the grieving to get a grip again, to reach out and re-engage. And it's not because people around you don't care or want intentionally to leave you behind, but it's easy to feel that way. People can only hold on to grief with you for so long before their hands begin to cramp.

This can be maddening for those who feel that, on top of their loss, they're facing a secondary loss of the world they knew before. Of course we want to go back and to pretend all is well but it's like rebuilding a sandcastle after it's been knocked down. Oh, friend—it'll never be what it was.

If you find yourself in this place of starting to get back on your feet, I wish that we could go walk the marshes and breathe salt air together. I wish we could go to Orchard House and stand by Lizzie's melodeon and talk about how everything has changed. Talk about how this wasn't the story we wanted to tell.

And as we stand there and see the portrait of Lizzie, the only image of her we even have, you'd turn and look to see a stoic portrait of Louisa on the adjacent wall. She looks dignified but weary. She didn't love the painting; to her, it seemed that she looked too old and tired and haggard. She told people that she looked like "a relic from the Boston fire." One day, when my friend Deborah was leading a tour and told that fact to a group, a woman said, "I don't see that at all. I see grit and determination. I see a survivor."

By the time Louisa May Alcott was has become internationally famous for writing, she had been sick for a very long while. The mercury had taken its toll on her body; with that sort of poisoning, bones start to deteriorate, arthritis sets in, and the body generally gives way to weakness easily. Louisa struggled a lot with a tired frame and worn-out hands, which was problematic, given the fact that she was making a living by writing.

Nevertheless, as time went on, she was preparing at last to finally tell the story of her sisters. Perhaps it took her ten years to write this magnum opus because, as a writer, she needed things to simmer for a while. Since writing about one's family in their ordinary life wasn't popular nor particularly marketable at that time, it seemed that the project was always on the back burner.

For as long as she could remember, Louisa had been writing fairy stories and thrillers and other pieces of fiction, but the story that haunted her and that would become the most impactful was the story of four young girls, growing up and making their way in the world. She was earning a few hundred dollars a year and working hard toward her goal of earning $1,000 annually. While that may not seem like much to us, by comparison, her father made about $100 a year at the peak of his academic career as the superintendent of schools for Concord. Louisa was the breadwinner and knew it full well.

Marmee was getting older, and Bronson had never made a sizable wage, and Anna was with John. May, who had not yet fallen in love, was doing her best, but Louisa's prolific ability to write stories meant that she was the one with the most financial promise.

Sometimes, when I go through her journals, I find side notes that she added later on. Annotations of sorts. She offered her commentary years and years after the events took place and went back in her journal to comment on particular seasons. At one point, when she was desperately hustling to make ends meet for the family, she wrote the simple note, "Too much work for one young woman. No wonder she broke down." Her ten-years-older self knew what the younger Louisa was still learning: life was taking a toll, and she could not afford to stop writing.

After successfully publishing a few shorter stories, something new started to happen in the broader culture that would change the trajectory of Louisa's life forever.

Girls started to read.

Up until this point, only boys went to school and were educated. It wasn't considered necessary for a woman to write. In fact, it was considered bad for their health. Sure, letter writing was permissible, but if a woman was being paid to write, it fell under the category of "brain work" and was not acceptable for women to do. One of the reasons Bronson Alcott lost his job over and over again was that he was willing to educate girls. He was, in that way, ahead of his time.

As the school system in the United States started to shift toward educating young girls, a conundrum emerged: they didn't have anything to read. Most of the stories that were in circulation at this point were written by men and for men and they also were about men. There were very few examples of women represented in literature in thoughtful and honest ways, so a publisher reached out to Louisa to ask if she would consider writing a story for girls.

"Mr. N. wants a girls' story, and I begin 'Little Women.'
Marmee, Anna, and May all approve my plan. So I plod
away, though I don't enjoy this sort of thing. Never liked

*girls or knew many, except my sisters; but our queer plays
and experiences may prove interesting, though I doubt it."*

She later added one small annotation: "Good Joke."

And isn't that just the way? We never know exactly how
things will turn out. We have no clue what tomorrow will
bring and we jump to so many conclusions, especially when
we are in the thick of a dark season. In my days of talking to
Jill and applying for jobs, I never would have guessed that I
would be able to breathe again. It was all-consuming and the
idea that peace would ever come—let alone healing—seemed
impossible.

So much of the time, when I'm annoyed with people in the
Bible for being, well, human, it's because they're acting like
they don't know what's coming next. And I sit here, reading
about their choices, and I judge them for their stupidity. Why
are the Hebrews complaining in the wilderness? Don't they
know the promised land is coming? Can't they just get over
themselves?

But when you're right in the middle of a whole lot of fog,
it is, not shockingly, difficult to see where you're going. All
of those months of processing grief had taken their toll, and
I found myself wandering around, jumping to conclusions
and deciding that Jesus wasn't for me. But when I decided
that afternoon on the phone with Pastor Bobby to just say
exactly what I was thinking and feeling, the world didn't end.
I remember taking a walk shortly after that phone call and
fighting it out with Jesus. I marched against the frigid late-
winter air and could feel myself on the edge of all of my ugly
emotions. I felt forgotten and unseen. I was sure that he was
teasing when he promised that he'd provide.

I was sick of hearing stories of people who job searched
and found something after two months and still called it a
harrowing experience.

I was tired of watching other people move on quickly from their grief and feeling like I was stuck in quicksand, unable to pull myself out.

And don't even get me started on the complaints that I regularly heard on social media about how annoying it was to have a job. I would have given my arms and legs for a steady paycheck.

They were not the ones having nightmares and feeling like they were going to throw up when it was time to pay utilities. And this is one of the trickier things that I do have to say about the process of losing: You have very little patience for the seeming ordinary-ness of everyone else's story. It is easy to give in to cynicism and believe that you are alone and everyone sucks. It is easy to give up on the struggle to see the silver lining. And in that moment on that cold walk in March, I was through with the stupid silver lining. I had mustered all I could and tried to be faithful and patient, but I was very over it, and in my anger I said to God, "Listen to me. I need you to show up or I am walking away."

Yes, I understand that telling God to "show up" is not theologically sound because he's everywhere always, but I need you to know that I was in a place where I couldn't pretend that all was well, and it felt like the equivalent of locking the door, pulling the blinds, and saying, "Neither of us leaves until we figure this crap out."

The Psalms are full of language where David has absolutely had it with niceties. He cries out to God with words of groaning and pain. In Psalm 38, he writes:

> "I am feeble and crushed;
>   I groan because of the tumult of my heart ...
>
> "My heart throbs; my strength fails me,
>   and the light of my eyes—it has also gone from me."
>   (Psalm 38:8, 10)

He doesn't hide his internal struggle at all, and in a lot of ways, David gave me the go-ahead to get real with God.

I was all in to walk all out. I was done being nice, and I needed to know that some kind of shift was coming. I imagined it was going to be a job interview or a magical mystery check or some other "hang in there, pal" kind of message. But what I got was a simple nudge to call my friend Anna. We hadn't talked in literal months, and she was up to her elbows in rowdy boys, but when she picked up the phone, it felt like a lifeline. I told her everything and how mad I was and how lost I felt, and by the end of the conversation I was back in my apartment, sitting on the stairs, enormously sad.

I thought I was angry about losing my job, but it all came down to this: I was very sad. As I previously mentioned, anger is often a front for sadness and I would venture to guess that most of the time when we think we're really angry, if we take a deep breath and let our mind slow down for just a moment, we will find that we are very sad. These last few years have given us plenty of opportunity to lose and lose and lose some more. Of course we're very sad.

And it's not just that. I think that we also feel very sad because we think that the stories we are now telling are somehow a major letdown. We thought that the years to come would be bright and beautiful and good, but we were met with isolation and loneliness and despair. Those of us on the verge of chronic anxiety or depression were launched head-first into a space with no coping mechanisms. We couldn't just drop in at a moment's notice on a friend without calling in advance or putting on a mask. The logistics suddenly felt very complicated.

No matter where you stand on the topic of how things could've been handled or should have been handled, I think that we can all agree that we were so, so tired.

After that phone call with Anna, I called my friend Audrey.

She was a faithful friend who was close with Anna and me in our graduate school years. We all used to be tied to our Greek and Hebrew textbooks, trying to figure out what was coming next. I watched them fall in love and start families and move around and serve in their local churches. I trusted them and needed their words of encouragement and honest straight-talk. We had been in the trenches together for years, and what I cherish about my afternoon of feeling my anger and sadness is that they were both there.

I do not remember what each of these dear women said to me. But I do remember that they were very present and listened and did not try to fix me. They did not try to offer me some sort of resolution to my lament and loneliness. They did not try to force theology down my throat or reprimand me for getting so angry at God. What they heard on the other side of that phone call was not a project but a person. And they treated me as that and it made all the difference because I desperately needed someone else to believe that Jesus was still kind, and that's exactly what they did. In fact, they were the example of Jesus' kind love for me by joining in my pain and messiness and never hesitating for a moment to do that. The fellowship and friendship they provided was preaching to me that God really did make us for community, and we really do need others to point us toward faith.

We desperately need community. And God is going to use people to bring us back to himself when we find ourselves drifting out to sea. I read a lot of articles about those who have abandoned their faith or deconstructed it in some way, and one of the threads that seems to be consistently woven throughout all of them is this: so many people suffered in silence by themselves. They had questions about their faith and they didn't know where to turn, and so they turned inward and found themselves leading a double life in the worst kind of way.

I do not believe that someone who deconstructs and no longer considers him- or herself self to be a Christian necessarily sets out to do that. Most of the time, there is some sort of trauma or grief or sadness that jolts them out of the repetitive motions they found themselves in and the patterns that they had found comfortable. The aftermath of that jolt draws them away from God rather than toward him. And when one thing starts to unravel, everything comes undone. A lot of the time, when this person is a Christian leader, they are not part of an intimate community where someone can challenge them or ask them the hardest questions. Instead, they feel that they must resolve things themselves and without the support of others who are in different places in their faith walk, and it's no wonder that they then decide that they cannot continue to pursue these beliefs.

As a woman with a seminary degree, who happens to love women in the local church, I cannot tell you how many times I have heard people comment on how much they cannot stand women's ministry. They say that it is shallow and judgmental and catty and full of gossip. There are about a million reasons to dislike this particular area of focus in the local church, but most of the time when somebody airs their grievances, the first question I want to ask them is:

"Who hurt you?"

The old adage that hurt people hurt people is true, and the church is no exception. And if you find yourself in a place of nodding along, I want you to know you are not alone in the questions you are asking and the concerns that you have. The church is full of broken people, some of whom do terrible things to one another and that don't reflect who Christ calls us to be. It is no wonder that there seems to be a whole lot of controversy around the people of God. We have never been put together and we almost always drop the ball at some—or several—points.

But take heart! Because the timeline of God's big story of the kingdom does not start, nor end, with us.

And while that might make us feel insignificant and small, it's actually freeing because we are not the ones who run the timeline nor are we the ones who call the shots. And while at times that feels threatening, it ultimately is a comfort because we can keep handing things back to the Author and Perfecter of our faith.

The reason that Anna's and Audrey's phone calls were so pivotal for me was not because they reinforced my reality, but because they reminded me of the truer reality. I was able to hear from somebody who had a perspective outside of my own, and they were able to speak gently and kindly to me in my struggle and invite me to look up for a moment.

Their actions reminded me that there are a whole lot of things I don't see going on, but they are all pointing back to this strange and wonderful story told by a God who can handle our anger and grief. And not only can he handle it; he can carry it. In the Old Testament, there are passages that use an image of God lifting or carrying his people. They say things like...

> "... and in the wilderness, where you have seen how the
> LORD your God carried you, as a man carries his son,
> all the way that you went until you came to this place"
> (Deuteronomy 1:31)

When we are heavy and cannot possibly get up again, we have a God that doesn't just cheer for us or give us advice. He actually lifts us up and carries us through the devastation that we are overcome by. And just like Galatians 6:2 encourages us to bear one another's burdens, and so fulfill the law of Christ, we are carried by God as we carry one another.

I hung up after these phone calls and knew that very little had changed, but I saw I was part of a bigger narrative and believed, even for a split second, that perhaps God would eventually "show up." I didn't feel rainbows and butterflies, and the sky did not part (in fact, it was very lousy weather that matched my own ennui) but, much to my shock, I saw that I'd put one foot in front of the other with the help of the Lord and these dear friends.

I'm not going to tell you that my grief evaporated, but my posture shifted from "I need it to be fine" to "I'm going to trust that eventually, it will be different." My heart was weary, but somehow, Jesus was still there, even if it seemed that he wasn't saying much.

I think we all really just want a good story to tell in the aftermath of loss. We want the happy ending and the "aha" moment, and when it doesn't happen we feel very disappointed. Mostly, because we are left with what we had before and what we had before wasn't particularly what we wanted.

It's no wonder that Louisa was so very convinced that *Little Women* would be a flop.

> *"June—Sent twelve chapters of '[Little Women]' to Mr. N. He thought it dull; so do I. But [I] work away ... for lively, simple books are very much needed for girls, and perhaps I can supply the need."*

I love that Louisa's primary goal was to supply a need. She had her gifts and was determined to use them for a greater good. And maybe that's what pulls us out of our self-centered fog at times—offering our stories to someone else. Recognizing that there are others out there, too and we are not only here for ourselves.

For much of his kingship, David wanted to build a temple. He had grand plans of building a majestic and beautiful structure that would honor and glorify God. And ultimately, his heart was to put plans into motion to allow it to happen, but he was held back by his own sins and selfishness and deceit. At a certain point he realized that if the temple was ever going to be built, it wouldn't be during his lifetime. In his dying years, as his body grew weak and feeble, he made sure that the supplies and plans necessary were handed off to his son, Solomon. And while we might see that and think it is a father taking care of his son, it is actually a king relinquishing his throne with humility and the foresight that it takes to lead well. Solomon knew this about his father David and said:

> "Blessed be the LORD, the God of Israel, who with his hand
> has fulfilled what he promised with his mouth to David
> my father, saying, 'Since the day that I brought my people
> out of the land of Egypt, I chose no city out of all the tribes
> of Israel in which to build a house, that my name might be
> there, and I chose no man as prince over my people Israel;
> but I have chosen Jerusalem that my name may be there,
> and I have chosen David to be over my people Israel.' Now
> it was in the heart of David my father to build a house
> for the name of the LORD, the God of Israel. But the LORD
> said to David my father, 'Whereas it was in your heart
> to build a house for my name, you did well that it was
> in your heart. Nevertheless, it is not you who shall build
> the house, but your son who shall be born to you shall
> build the house for my name.' Now the LORD has fulfilled
> his promise that he made. For I have risen in the place
> of David my father and sit on the throne of Israel, as the
> LORD promised, and I have built the house for the name of
> the LORD, the God of Israel." (2 Chronicles 6:4-10)

We see this foresight also in the life of Moses. He had led the Hebrews out of slavery and into the wilderness where they wandered for 40 years. He had witnessed wonders and fought battles and carried so many losses and wins in his time as one of the greatest fathers of the faith, but as his eyes grew tired and his earthly existence came to an end, he knew that he needed to provide Joshua his successor with wisdom. Because of some of his own shortcomings, Moses would not see the promised land except from a distance as he stood on a mountain and took it in. This was an opportunity for him to become bitter against God for not letting him see the fruit of all of his labor, but in his old age he had become wise and knew that the plan for God's people was much greater than the length of his earthly years.

> "So Moses continued to speak these words to all Israel. And he said to them, 'I am 120 years old today. I am no longer able to ego out and come in. The LORD has said to me, "You shall not go over this Jordan." The LORD your God himself will go over before you. He will destroy these nations before you, so that you shall dispossess them, and Joshua will go over at your head, as the LORD has spoken."
> (Deuteronomy 31:1-3)

So he poured into Joshua, and he gave him everything he needed to succeed. Generations later, David would do the same thing. These were not men who were after their own reputation being exalted, but they were more than willing to play a small part in a greater story that God was telling.

It takes a God-given sort of wisdom for someone to willingly do what these great men of faith did. And while the world will tell you that being a leader is about being number one and having it all together and never doubting God for a moment, we see when we read the story of Moses that he doubted God often (see, for example, Numbers 11:21-23) and when we look at the narrative of David, we see that he was regularly upset with the Lord (for example, in 1 Samuel 6:8). But both of them kept coming back to God because they knew that he was not done with the story that was unfolding.

I wonder what Moses and David would have to say if they could go back and annotate their own stories the way that

Louisa did? Would they see their own faithlessness and add a sarcastic comment? Would they cringe over the foolish decisions that they made or have compassion for their younger selves who were so eager and misplaced in their motives?

What we do know is that when Solomon dedicated the temple, he presented it as the work of his father because he knew that in David's heart, he was the instigator and therefore deserved credit. And something else really interesting happens here: David's heart and his motives are what the Lord remembers, too. He gives David credit for building the temple, even though you could easily argue that David didn't. And that's because God sees into our hearts and what matters to him most is not the work we do with our hands, but how our intentions are set (1 Samuel 16:7).

I think that in his kindness, God meets us in our anger and sadness because it's all we can offer. When we are stripped down and left with nothing impressive and a whole lot of feelings, God is not put off and doesn't pull away. Rather, he moves in close and reveals that it was never about the cinematic storyline or the Hallmark moment. It was about taking the next step forward in regular life and welcoming him into it.

Louisa thought she'd make her money with sensationalism and drama, but it turns out, the story she deemed dull was the one that was anything but. It's almost like the ordinary leads the way.

CHAPTER 9

What Cannot Be Lost

As I'm sure you're well aware if you've heard the story of Louisa at all, she's about to come into some money and pretty outrageous success. And, if I'm honest, I don't want to tell you about it.

I don't want to tell you about her success in light of what we have been discussing because the theme of this book is loss and losing things and she is about to gain. A lot. I cannot stress to you how insanely wealthy she is about to be after decades of struggle and poverty.

Louisa was just as shocked as anyone when, while standing in the dining room, she received some mail: an envelope from her publisher with a whole lot more money than she was expecting. It turns out that *Little Women* was a runaway hit and what she had thought was boring and ordinary and common-place in fact offered something that everyone needed in a time of post-Civil War unrest: relatability.

There is no magic formula to get a book to sell. If I knew one, I would tell all of my friends in publishing and we would see hit after hit. But I can tell you as someone who does work in this industry that success is honestly due to a strange combination of things. Good writing helps, and a great publisher helps even more. But it really rests on the audience and if they're ready to receive the message of the book.

Little Women came out in 1868, just three years after the Civil War ended. The United States was in the Reconstruction Era, and it took a tremendous amount of work to rebuild what had been pulled apart. Everyone had lost someone or multiple someones, and they were desperate for some sort of comfort. They knew that they were not the only ones in a new season of growth, and this book offered insight into the human condition in the form of a story about family.

While the plot is about the March girls' coming of age, as they figure out what they love and learn to care for one another well, it's also a story of tremendous loss. Beth is massively understated and yet the loss of her cannot be over-estimated. She represented to so many readers the sister or the brother or the friend they once had and lost too soon. I can tell you, after giving so many tours in Orchard House, that Louisa was the one who forged the path. She was the one who made a way to talk about grief on the world stage in a way that hadn't really been done before.

She went first, and it shook the world.

There were plenty of books that were being written at this point, and *Little Women* could have easily slipped into the wasteland of books that were published and never made it further than one printing. But it didn't. The book was originally written in two volumes and many international editions still separate it into two books. The first volume ended with Meg's wedding. Everyone was happy, and Jo was unmarried, and Amy had never been to Europe, and Beth was still alive. And this is one of the most important and interesting parts of the story for me, because I believe Louisa had very intentionally rearranged the timeline here.

In reality, Lizzie died and the family was plunged into sorrow as they moved into Orchard House. They took her things with them to a home she never fully lived in. They missed her in the hallways and bedrooms when they brought out the dolls and costumes and quilts. They ached for her to walk through the door again, just like when she was still alive and they were making Orchard House their own, choosing wallpaper and arranging the floor plan.

As I related earlier, not long after they moved into Orchard House, John Pratt and Anna were married in the parlor in a small but full ceremony performed by Marmee's brother. Their love was a bright spot in an otherwise dark season of loss, and it gave the family something to celebrate, which they were desperate for. It was a simple ceremony and a joyful occasion, but there was a void felt when Lizzie didn't see her sister off or dance with the others, laughing and pushing her hair out of her face, out of breath.

And so I don't blame Louisa for making sure Beth was at Meg's wedding.

She just wanted to tell a good story. She just wanted the grief to go away for a moment, even if it was only for the March family and not her own.

The success of *Little Women* came on slowly at first, and then it was like a full-moon high tide, flooding over. After the first volume was released, children from all over the country wrote in because they desperately wanted to know what happened to the little women. Understandably, they wanted Jo to end up with Laurie, and Amy to become a famous artist, and Beth to make her way in the world as an accomplished musician. But Louisa knew the truth, and it was something that she had to face as she turned her attention to the second half of the story.

In the second volume, after the wedding, the March girls grew up. Childhood in so many ways was over, and adulthood brought with it the harsh realities of the world around them. Meg struggled with finances and a deep desire for more when she had very little. Amy wanted to be a world-renowned artist and came to the realization that she was the one who would have to call it quits and talk herself out of chasing fame. Beth got sick again, and in the 40th chapter of *Little Women*, titled, "The Valley of the Shadow," she finally succumbed to scarlet fever and the complications that it had wrought in her body. Louisa wrote tenderly, as if the wounds were still fresh, even though her own dear Lizzie had died ten years prior. And isn't that just the way that grief works? I can tell you the exact feelings that went through my body over a decade after some of the heartbreak from my twenties. Two years out from Jill's death, I can still feel the cold marsh air on my cheeks, which turns them red. Our bodies remember, and Louisa's was no exception. She remembered the sweetness of her sister and the kindness in her eyes and the absolute devastation that it brought upon the family when she left first.

Recently, someone was leading a tour at Orchard House, and there was a small girl who grew very upset when Beth's story was told because she didn't think that Beth had died. Her parents were apologetic and reminded her that they had just recently read the story and that Beth had, in fact, died. "No!" the girl said. "In the book it says, 'And Beth was well at last.'"

She's not wrong. Out of the mouth of babes, I suppose. Louisa did write Beth's death as some sort of a resurrection, and I believe it's because she truly felt deep down that this story is not the end.

When Louisa's first check came in for the second volume of *Little Women*, it was for over $7,000—over one million by today's standard. And the checks kept coming in, to the shock and delight of the Alcotts.

They had a furnace installed so that each room had heat, and more lavish carpeting and furniture were purchased. The luxuries that they had so long desired and had not been able to afford were at their fingertips.

When we find ourselves coming out of a season of great loss, it is easy to feel as though our troubles are behind us. Of course, there's also a good percentage of us that have had enough loss in our lives that we are immediately suspicious of any kind of uptick in morale. We wait for the other shoe to drop, feeling as though our momentary joy is nothing more than exactly that: momentary. We are wounded by what we have lost, and it's hard to push forward with any semblance of steadiness when things have been trembling for so long.

Perhaps you are in that space of peeking out from behind closed shutters, trying to decide if it's safe to come out.

Can God really be trusted again with our desires and hopes and prayers?

Didn't he leave us hanging before?

Sometimes the most vulnerable statement I can make is telling God that I trust him. Shortly before Jill got sick, I wrote in my journal that "I trust you" to Jesus because I really did feel that way. But as things started to deteriorate, I found myself not wanting to write words like that anymore. I had more hurt than I had ever thought possible, and I was reluctant to provide any other opportunities for Jesus to let me down.

One afternoon, I decided that I needed to write those three words again and again as a form of making myself remember the truth that God can be trusted.

The first time I wrote "I Trust You," I felt a tightness in my chest because the last thing I wanted to do was willingly hand him my heart after feeling so very bruised.

This is what I love about our grief and our God: he carries us through it and provides a safe harbor even though he feels the loss even more greatly than we ever could.

Only God truly knows the cost of death. He's the only one who was ever around before it who lived to tell the tale after it. Since the very start, we have died and while we believe in the hope of resurrection to new life, death saturates the whole world around us. There is no escaping it. The other shoe absolutely will drop.

Anna's husband, John, got sick. It was sudden, and within about two weeks, he was dead. He left behind two young sons, and, together with their newly widowed mother, they moved back into Orchard House. Louisa and Anna shared a room and a nursery for Freddy and Johnny was added onto the home.

> "January, 1871: Began to write a new book, "Little Men," that John's death may not leave A[nna] and the dear little boys in want. John took care that they should have enough while the boys are young, and worked very hard to have a little sum to leave, without a debt anywhere.

> "In writing and thinking of the little lads, to whom I must be a father now, I found comfort for my sorrow..."

Louisa stepped in to make sure that Anna and the boys never had to question if they would be free from poverty. Within two weeks of the announcement that *Little Men* was on the way, over 30,000 pre-orders had been made, and when the book was finally launched, that number had risen to 50,000. While Anna was then able to afford to purchase a house and live comfortably on her own with her sons, I can't help but think of that first year after John's death when she was sharing a room with her sister, just as if they were children again.

I imagine that Louisa would walk in absolutely exhausted and collapse onto the bed and ask Anna how the day had been. They would have delighted in the boys and mourned over how much things had turned out so very differently than they'd imagined as young girls.

Louisa had accomplished everything there really was to accomplish as a writer. At one point, she was the highest paid author of her time, and the success she achieved was truly unparalleled. Yet, loss continued to plague her.

She paid for May to go to Europe and take art lessons. May fell in love with a young man named Ernest, and they were married for two years before she gave birth to a little girl. Louisa had been demanding a niece all along and was overcome with satisfaction when she heard the news. She longed to go to Paris and be with the new mother, especially since the little niece was named Louisa May.

But with all of the success and riches possible, the Alcotts still felt the sting of more trouble as they were reacquainted with the valley of the shadow all over again.

> *"Wednesday, Jan 31st.—A dark day for us. A telegram from Ernest ... tells us 'May is dead' ... I was not surprised, and read the hard words as if I knew it all before ...*
>
> *"The dear baby may comfort Ernest, but what can comfort us? It is the distance that is so hard, and the thought of so much happiness ended so soon. 'Two years of perfect happiness' May called these married years, and said, 'If I die when baby comes, don't mourn, for I have had as much happiness in this short time as many in twenty years.' She wished me to have her baby and her pictures. A very precious legacy! Rich payment for the little I could do for her. I see now why I lived,—to care for May's child and not leave Anna all alone."*

Ernest decided to send his and May's daughter, by then nicknamed Lulu, to Concord to live with the family. Louisa, who never married or had children of her own, cared for little Lulu until she herself died a few years later.

***

Over and over again in Scripture, the people of God are told to remember. Most notably, the Israelites were commanded to remember what God had done for them. And it wasn't just a highlight reel. He wanted them to remember all of it.

Remember the parting of the Red Sea and the provision of manna in the wilderness, yes. But also remember that you were slaves and that all hope was lost. Remember that you were abused and neglected and left for dead. Remember that you only had the clothes on your back and you fled so quickly that the bread didn't have time to rise. Remember that your loved ones died in battle.

There is holiness in remembering because it recognizes that our stories are not only the mountaintops but the valleys, too. We have all wandered through the valley of the shadow, and it's something we not only have to remember but something we couldn't forget if we tried.

A lot of people out there preach that because Jesus brings life and hope and love into our lives, we are nearest to him when we experience those things. When a child is born or wedding vows are exchanged or something terrific happens. But when we take that line of belief to its ultimate conclusion, it ends with caricatures of those things.

Suddenly, our team winning a football game or a check coming in the mail is equal to the goodness of God. So it is no wonder that when things go poorly or bad news comes, we believe that God is no longer good. We believe that he forgot us and chose instead someone with a better story to tell.

This is what I desperately want you to know: you are, right now, in the best possible position to be loved by God.

It doesn't matter what you have or what you had, what you gained or what you lost.

It doesn't matter what triumphs of profession or moments of victory preceded this.

And it doesn't matter what's coming down the road, either.

All we have is this one hilarious, ordinary, heartbreaking, very human life.

He doesn't accept us on the basis of anything other than what we are and his kindness is not being withheld but it's sometimes obstructed by the fog that surrounds us in seasons of devastation and long bouts of sorrow. The world we live in is just as broken now as it was in the 1800s. After extensive loss and heartache, and maybe even deconstruction, it can seem as though our own civil war has been waged, but maybe there is a moment coming for each of us that points to reconstruction.

The reason that David and Joshua and Moses and so many others died in peace was because they saw that they were only a small part of a much larger picture. Louisa knew that she was not long for this world and she saw to it that her family would find rest long after she did. She understood that there are overlapping timelines and when one thing ends, something else is probably beginning.

There's a man in John 5 who has been paralyzed for his whole life—38 years. He found himself at the pool of Bethesda, where those who were in need of healing would gather. It was believed that when the water was stirred, there were angels nearby and if you got in the water first you could be miraculously healed. But he was sick and tired and couldn't get to the water quick enough to be healed.

> "When Jesus saw him lying there and knew that he had already been there a long time, he said to him, 'Do you want to be healed?' The sick man answered him, 'Sir, I have no one to put me into the pool when the water is stirred up, and while I am going another steps down before me.' Jesus said to him, 'Get up, take up your bed, and walk.' And at once the man was healed, and he took up his bed and walked." (John 5:6-9)

Jesus brought healing to him right where he was, and so a man who was unable to move without assistance was able to stand and walk and it was a dang surprise to everyone. Later on, Jesus was at the temple, and so was the man so Jesus sought him out. In verses 13 and 14, it says:

> "Now the man who had been healed did not know who it was, for Jesus had withdrawn, as there was a crowd in the place. Afterward Jesus found him in the temple and said to him, 'See, you are well! Sin no more, that nothing worse may happen to you.'"

I always thought this was an ominous statement that Jesus makes here. "That nothing worse may happen to you" feels like something that's not so positive. But let's take a closer look. What Jesus is suggesting here is that there are worse things than being physically unwell. And he is not just healing this man so that he can walk but so that he can find true healing for his soul.

Time and time again, when people come to Christ, he ministers to their bodies and their souls as well. He cares for the whole of us—not just the outside. He wants this man to live a life in which he is spiritually walking with God. In a similar way, Jesus cares deeply for our souls when we are sick or loving others who are sick.

I wish I could give you a cure for death and the hell it wreaks in our lives. I wish that I could say that Jesus always heals us physically on this side of heaven. But, although I can't, the reality is that in some wild way, Jill is fully healed in body and soul even as you turn these pages. Because our God is not just God of the physical world but the eternal one, and he brings new life to us that lasts long after our final breath here on earth. He showed up not just to bring us good food or fix our ailments but to settle peace into our very hearts and souls with his presence. He gives us that inheritance that doesn't rust or decay because we are his and he loves us tremendously—all of us. The dark and dangerous and deathly ways of this world do not stop Jesus from rescuing us over and over again.

I hate every day that Jill is dead. And that I cannot call her or hear her voice in real time anymore. I hate that I'm still here and she's not, but I know that she still lives on in the memories we carry and the jokes we make and every little way she pointed us to what is good and true.

I finally have come to a place of exhale knowing that much like Beth, Jill is well at last. She is more alive than she ever has been and she is in the constant company of Christ. And by his grace, when I come to God with whatever trivial sort of thoughts or feelings I have, and I draw near to him, I know that Jill is even nearer to him and it is good.

What I experience in part, she knows fully.

***

At the end of every tour, we find ourselves standing in Bronson's study. One winter afternoon, a woman asked how we became a museum. We stood in silence for a moment with the floor creaking underneath us, and I shifted my weight as a smile came across my face.

"Well," I began, "there was a woman named Margaret Sidney living next-door and she was an author, too. When the Alcotts moved out, this house sat empty for a very long time, and she was determined to make sure it could be honored well. She wrote letters to all of the women's leagues in the United States, explaining that she wanted to buy the house and turn it into a literary house museum. Slowly, funds came in from nearly every state in the Union, and she was able to purchase Orchard House. We opened our doors in 1911 and have been welcoming guests from all over the world ever since."

We stood there for a moment, taking in the history and the passion and the community that it took to allow us to stand in that room among so many rich artifacts, and then, one by one, everyone left the study, heading off to dinner or a hike or the long road back home.

So, what do we do now? When the tour is over and we're left on our own to find the next right step? How do we push forward?

Perhaps it's by opening our mouths and telling our stories. Calling a trusted friend or mentor or pastor and saying, "I need to tell this to someone else." Many times over these years, I've needed someone else to know what was racing through my mind, not so they could save me but so that they could see me and preach back to me until I remember that Jesus sees me even more.

It has taken years of counseling and processing and prayer to have arrived here, but it's going to be something I carry with me the rest of my life. I will grow old without Jill, and we'll never go to Disneyland, and that will be the story I'll walk out without her.

Jesus and I are still working things out, one mile at a time. Sometimes, we barely make it to the parking lot before I start protesting. Other times, I linger in the living room where I used to swear in anger over these losses and I find myself swaying side to side, almost like we're in a slow dance. It's as if I can sense his closeness. I am tired, but I am held, and it's my prayer for you to sense that as well. I keep showing up, and he never fails to be present. I try to bring my most honest self, even when I feel ungrateful or suspicious or ridiculously insecure. And he meets me, every dang time, right in the dust or the desert or on the dance floor.

We are in process—always fighting for light. But there has not been a moment when he walked out or gave up or refused to look me in the eye. In his kindness, God has been the

WHAT CANNOT BE LOST

person that I cannot lose, even when I am so sure all hope is lost. He stays—isn't that the sweetest sort of news?

When the last tour heads home, I walk from room to room, turning off lights. First, it's the kitchen, where they gathered and swept up and Louisa would simmer her stories while she cooked. Then, it's the dining room, where Lizzie's melodeon sits quietly in the corner. Next, it's the parlor, where Anna and John said, "I do" and audiences sat during theatrical performances.

After that, I head upstairs and close up Louisa's bedroom: I pass the bed where she recovered from her illness, and I smile softly as I watch the candlelight flicker on the desk where she wrote *Little Women*.

Then it's time for May's room, where I turn off the lamps next to photos of Lulu and her father, Ernest. And then, it's across the hall to Marmee's room, where they added the nursery for Freddy and Johnny—my favorite wallpaper in the house, in case you're wondering.

Finally, I make my way to the study again, where I take a last look at the books on the shelves. Early editions of Louisa's work and the family copy of *Pilgrim's Progress* sit with notes inside from the members of the Alcott family, and I am reminded: others saw a rundown house, pieced together over centuries. But Louisa knew what I now sense to be the strange reality of death and redemption; even with the heartbreak that has filled these spaces, one day, the stories of days that felt most harrowing will be the ones that people show up for and ask to be told over and over again.

Your grief is not the very end of the story, friend.

You will live out this day and as many days as the Lord has for you, and you will not be alone in that feeling that there's a little something missing, nor will you be alone in lamenting that reality. Until we meet Jesus face to face, we will always be missing something or someone. We will always be aching for a forever that is whole and resolved and free from tears and the sting of death.

But for now? We keep going. We keep carrying one another and holding each other's arms up. We keep telling Jesus exactly where we're at and coming to him with what Vivian Mabuni calls "open hands and a willing heart." We will keep on moving forward because we are, as Christians, not those who mourn with no hope (1 Thessalonians 4:13).

No, we hold on to hope, even in the darkest of dark. Not because it erases our pain, but because it points to a better end, not the bitter end.

Her last note. To Mrs. Bond. February 8, 1888.

"Dear Auntie,—I little knew what a sweet surprise was in store for me when I wrote to you yesterday.

"As I awoke this morning my good Doctor L. came in with the lovely azalea, her round face beaming through the leaves like a full moon.

"It was very dear of you to remember me, and cheer up my lonely day with such a beautiful guest.

"It stands beside me on Marmee's work-table, and reminds me tenderly of her favorite flowers; and among those used at her funeral was a spray of this, which lasted for two weeks afterward, opening bud after bud in the glass on her table, where lay the dear old 'Joseph May' hymn book, and her diary with the pen shut in as she left it when she last wrote there, three days before the end, 'The twilight is closing about me, and I am going to rest in the arms of my children.'

"So you see I love the delicate flower, and enjoy it very much.

"I can write now, and soon hope to come out and see you for a few minutes, as I drive out every fine day, and go to kiss my people once a week for fifteen minutes.

"Slow climbing, but I don't slip back; so think up my mercies, and sing cheerfully, as dear Marmee used to do, 'Thus far the Lord has led me on!'

"Your loving Lu."

Afterword

How do you explain the companionship of your nearest friend? How do you tell others about how that person carried you and never failed and always knew exactly what to say? When I think about my journey toward becoming a Christian, it starts in simple enough ways: I was in my childhood bedroom, having heard about how Jesus was someone to be trusted and welcomed into my life in such a near way that I was welcoming him into my very heart. This sort of thing sounds more than a little strange, but I have found the richest parts of life to be that way.

So I'll say it like this: I was born into this world into a family and community that I grew up with and that nurtured me. I learned about the beauty of the world and the heartbreak of it, too. People got sick and lost faith in the goodness of living, and sometimes the car broke down or we ran low on resources.

But there was wonder, too: like watching the fireflies at my grandparents' house or running fast behind my sister in the backyard. Still, something seemed to be woven into all of it—a sort of thread that connected everything and stayed steady in the middle of upheaval.

I believed from a young age in Bible stories that told me about the creation of the world, but as I got older, I saw the ways that these seemingly distant stories about the ancient Near East somehow trickled into my own little existence. I read about how the world was touched by sin and death, and I got a taste of it with every argument or prideful jab or funeral. It was enough to make a small child feel very worried because life, it turns out, isn't forever.

But here's the wild thing about the Bible: it doesn't leave us in the mess but promises a better story that ends with new life and the truest redemption. For every broken piece, there is this sovereign God over all of it who feels tenderness and compassion and kindness—grace—for his people. Rather than staying at a distance, letting us suffer for the mistakes we make and the ways we hurt one another, he chooses over and over again to provide and to comfort and to stand in the gap, taking the consequences of our short-comings to bring us back into relationship with him. He chose to give up his very own Son, Jesus, who came down and put on flesh. Jesus— who could have had every worldly advantage and who carried the power of the divine—decided to show up like us, as a human person who felt feelings and witnessed the wonders and terrors of this place. And he resolved, in his very core, to do something about the brokenness; to stay and to love and to tell the truth, even though it cost him his life.

In John 15:13, it says, "Greater love has no one than this, that someone lay down his life for his friends". And when Jesus, who was the very embodiment of love and goodness and innocence showed up, people misunderstood his actions and twisted his words until some of them demanded that he die. Yet Jesus didn't fight back. He didn't beg to be spared or use his power to remove himself from the situation. Instead, he willingly laid down his life for his friends. In that time, people would offer a lamb or calf as a way to cover the cost of their imperfection in the presence of a perfect God. Jesus made an offering of himself, giving up his own life to pay the cost of his friends' flaws and failings so that they could enjoy life in the presence of God forever.

This is where believing comes in because it doesn't always feel easy to put trust in things we can't see. We call that faith.

When I feel so very small or insecure or that all hope is lost, I remember this part of the story: that, after he had died, Jesus came back. He rose again, and suddenly death and emptiness beyond wasn't the only option anymore. In an instant, someone had bridged the gap between spotless deity and broken humanity. And when we look to him, we have another way to live—one that doesn't involve measuring up or trying to be totally perfect or earning love.

Look around—the way of this world is ego and competence and social standing. But the way of following Jesus? It cannot be bought or earned—only received. Which means that when my heart is broken—again—or my world feels shaky when another war breaks out or another terrorist attack comes on the screen or a friend betrays me or I speak words that aren't kind—when I am in need of grace, it is always available. Grace is only found in the person of Jesus, who loved us enough to die in our place and come back again as if to say, Oh, is that the thing we were all worried about?

Even now, as I write these words, I cannot fully make sense of all the ways he has met me in my need. I know that I belong and that I am held, and that while I am a sinner that is no longer my primary identity, because Christ himself makes me new every single moment. As Oswald Chambers once said, "The Spirit of God brings justification with a shattering, radiant light, and I know that I am saved, even though I don't know how it was accomplished."

I know—this sort of way of existing sounds too good to be true; I can assure you it is not. I can tell you how God has met me in the darkest dark and steadied my anxious soul over and over again. I can tell you that I have watched in my dearest friends the transformation that only God can provide. I have seen the goodness shine through, and the world that we live in feels suddenly very small and dim when we get a glimpse of the eternity beyond us. And that's what keeps those who trust in Jesus steadfast and hopeful from generation to generation. This is why Christianity doesn't have a tendency to go away. Because we have found an answer to the questions this broken world keeps posing us, and he is called Jesus.

If you want to know more about this very good and very kind and very gracious God, reach out to me, or maybe tap on the shoulder of a friend who loves Jesus. Keep asking good questions and looking for light, and know that God's grace is as real as the rivers and deserts and mountains and the sea. It has always been and will be forever, and we get to watch it unfold in our lives. Thanks be to God.

Acknowledgments

I cannot thank the Wojtanowicz family enough for their gift of sharing Jill with me and being some of the very first to read these words and offer their blessing over them. They raised a good woman, and it is an honor to carry her stories forward together. Jill was so very loved and cared for and cherished to the very end in their home. Jill, we miss you every dang day. Thank you for how you lived. You were a gift, and others know Jesus better because of you. I can't wait to dance with you again.

Dan, you loved Jill from the start and selflessly honored her and fought for her and pursued her and delighted her every day that you could. She loved being your wife and laughing with you, constantly telling me how grateful she was for you and your love.

Gudim family, thank you for showing up and loving Dan and Jill and bringing Midwestern hospitality to the West Coast.

This book was carried by people near and far over hillsides and across rivers and through valleys.

Thank you to the friends who heard about this book and steadied me first. Grace P. Cho told me my voice mattered; Lisa Whittle let me know with grace and love that this wouldn't be simple; Kelsea Walkley listened and honored it with kindness; Tim and Ann Marton watched me get rejected and lose over and over again, but kept showing up and opening their arms and home and mouths to speak love. Kevin and Bailey Utecht let me cry and rant and celebrate, and opened their home (and shared their couch) to help restore my exhausted frame. Kristin Beattie sat with me while I processed and gave me good hugs. Clarissa Moll went first so I could join the ranks of those who cry a lot in public places over strange things. Alicia Lewis helped crack my tired heart wide open under the safe cover of counseling and spiritual direction. Amanda Williams sent text messages like life rafts and let me grieve well. Meredith King never stopped checking in and steadying me. KJ Ramsey and Erin Moon immediately got on board and went to bat for me— what a freakin' lineup.

Beth Barnard, your songs have been pointing me to Jesus for over a decade, and having your words open this book was the best possible gentle leading for these readers. You have walked through the valley over and over, and your testimony of honesty and questioning and hope brings me back to earth. Thank you for your friendship, willingness, and humor.

When I was worn, I called on Maggie Johnson, who fought for me; Rachael Wade, who prayed over me; Tasha Jun, who held me upright; Aarti Sequeira, who warmed me with kindness; Aliza Latta and Kaitlyn Bouchillon, who talked for hours about writing and angst and the treacherous waters of single lady vulnerability. Anna Westfall and Audrey Adkins talked me off of ledges. Bob and Nancy Stallard provided a respite at their cabin. Bre Lee spoke life and truth, and Jordan Delk never stopped showing up and covering me in prayer. Cathy Galli and Ed Howard, you brought me into the store, gave me the honor of friendship, and walked a lot of things out with me these years.

To my church oversight, thank you for investing in me and praying over these words and these readers. Bob, Nancy, Ann, Tim, Natalie, Karen, Jon, Maria, Julie, and Debbi, your companionship shows me that I'm not crazy when I say that community matters.

To the hordes of beloved friends who showed up during dark days and cannot be overlooked: Bea Lyons, my high school small-group girls (Maddy, Madelyn, Caroline, Susie, Taylor, Grace, Emily, Emma), Priscilla Chow, Flo/Josh/Sera Sage / Amelie Oakes, Brinn Weaver, Brooke Park, Taylor and Ashley Marton, Brittany and Cameron Casey, Jaleesa McCreary, Jeni Son, Susan Choe, Heather Korpi, Joelinda and Kyle Johnson, Marya Marsh, Amanda May, Laura Range, Sarah Bartley, Laura Gallant, Ali Bitzer, Corrine Grant, Megan Berger, Taylor Leonhardt, Ellie Holcomb, Jessie Strauss, Jamie Abbitt, Kristine Rego, Rachel Blazer, Sandra McCracken, Daphne Bamburg, Savannah Conner, Julie Warrenburg, Julie Lenocker, Natalie Crowson, Lourdes Gomez, Jamie Ivey, Leslie Wallace, The Ferrees, TJ Ono, Ellie Weiner, Tracey Westgate, Barb Harris, Moses Camacho, Jenna Williams, Melissa Moore, Jo Saxton, Melissa Tate, Ana Wrede, JJ Heller, Natalie Lloyd, Mary Miller, Debbie Kellogg, Patti Duncan-Rice, Laura Booz, Asheritah Ciuciu, Jasmine Turrubiartes, Sharon Hodde Miller, Susan Berthiaume, Rachel Cotton, Lissa Whitley, Dave and Marilyn Sweet, Paul and Marcia Sidmore, Tom and Lucita Zhou, the Richard and Enid Band, and all of the others I'm probably forgetting (and I will get so mad when I remember).

To my colleagues: thank you for your grace as I worked full time and wrote this book on weekends. Kathryn, Emily, Ashley, Judy T, Judy D, Duane, Amy, and Janis, you cared well and I'm so thankful.

To my family—Mom, Dad, Laura, Rick, Thomas, Maddy, CJ, Diana: thanks for your patience and prayers as I wrote this. And to Emma, Constance, Bonnie, Holly, Myra, GG, Izabel, and Jack: you give me so much joy. Sheesh.

Thank you to Austin Wilson and the crew at Wolgemuth for your stewardship, advocacy, and stalwart hope in the face of rough odds.

To the team at The Good Book Company—thank you for believing in this book. Brian, you have been the very best editor and caught the vision. Bethany and Abigail, I couldn't be in better hands for getting the word out about this book. Thank you for your care and joy and thoughtfulness.

Obviously, I want to thank my Orchard House family. You watched and waited with me, spending long hours in the guide room offering encouragement, facts about the Alcotts, accountability that has spurred me to tell the truth about Louisa well, and a lot of good stories about how this house really is special because of the people that fill it. You have changed how I see the world around me. Jan, Maria, Lis, Jessie, Iman, Megan, Dianne, Deborah, Anne, Jennie, and everyone else: you are the best group of "Little Women".

To Orchard House (I know, I am thanking a house), thank you for standing for so long and being home to all of us for so many years.

And finally, to Lu: you went first and told the story of Beth and we are forever changed. I really hope I meet you in Eternity—you'll never believe what we did with the place.